The Way, The Truth and The Life

Pupil's Book 3

Authors
Sr. Marcellina Cooney CP & Angela Edwards

Editorial Team
Hilda Bellamy, Marie Buonocore, Betty Conboy, Amette Ley,
Vicky Lord, Susan Lawless, Kerry Malone, Monica Walczak

Teachers' Enterprise in Religious Education Co. Ltd

Introduction

Welcome to this second edition of *The Way, the Truth and the Life* series. Let us think about what this title means.

It is Jesus who said: *"I am the Way, the Truth and the Life"*. So it is Jesus who shows us the **Way** to lead a good and happy life. He tells us the **Truth** about God and he gives us new **Life** in the sacraments.

As you progress through your lessons in Religious Education this year, you will learn about the Sacrament of Baptism, the Sacrament of Reconciliation and what it means to celebrate the Mass.

In addition, you will learn about the mystery of the Incarnation and the life of Jesus and what it means to be one of his close friends, a Christian.

Most of all you will come to see how important our friendship with Jesus is and how much it helps us as we grow up. This is the great strength of our faith.

I hope you will spend time every day with Jesus in prayer.

+Vincent Nichols

✠ Vincent Nichols
Archbishop of Westminster

Contents

1. The Christian Family

Know that we all belong to a family.
Think about how we can help our family.

The Holy Family

When Jesus was a little boy he lived with his parents, Mary and Joseph, in their house in Nazareth. Jesus loved his family very much and Mary and Joseph took very good care of him.

Jesus, Mary and Joseph did lots of things together. They played together, they ate their meals together, they prayed together and they helped each other with all the jobs that had to be done. They shared many happy times as a family, and some sad times too.

Activity

Listen to the account of Mary and Joseph taking Jesus to the Temple in Jerusalem for the feast of the Passover. (Teacher's Book page 21).

a) What do you think this event tells us about Jesus?

b) How do you think Jesus behaved when he returned to Nazareth with Mary and Joseph?

Our Family

We all belong to a family. Some of us belong to a big one and others to a small one. Your family is a gift to you from God. God gave you a family so that you would have people to take care of you and to love you. You do special things together just like Jesus did and you can probably think of lots of happy times you have shared.

Being part of a family is not always easy. There are times when we find it difficult: for example, when we argue with brothers or sisters, leave all the work to one person, or we are tired of having to share all the time. No family is perfect.

Activities

1. Draw a picture or put a photo of your family in the centre of a page. Write what you and your family enjoy doing together.

2. Choose one very special time that you and your family have enjoyed together. Create a 'Thank You' card and say why this time was so special.

Activity

3. Work in pairs. Can you help these families?
   a) Read each problem.
   b) Say what the difficulty is.
   c) Suggest a solution.

It's grandad's birthday. The family are having a celebration for him but Paul wants to go to his football practice with his friends.

Laura and Mario always argue about whose turn it is on the computer. Everyone else in their family is tired of listening to them quarrel.

At the end of the day, Samil's family relax in different ways: he goes out on his bike, his big sister is on her laptop and Dad reads the newspaper. But, Mum always seems to be in the kitchen washing and tidying up after supper.

The Family of the Church

Know what it means to belong to the family of the Church.
Reflect on how the family of the Church helps us.

The Church

As well as our own special family, we belong to another family. This family is made up of people known as Christians, people like us, who love God and who want to live as Jesus lived. It is a very big family and we have brothers and sisters in every country all over the world. We call this family the Catholic Church.

The family of the Church is so big that we cannot all meet together in the same place. Instead, we meet as a much smaller group in our parish family led by our parish priest. A parish is all the people in our Church family who live near each other.

Key Words

parish priest   bishop   Mass

The Diocese

The **Pope** is in charge of the whole Catholic Church, the parishes and dioceses all over the world.

A **bishop** is in charge of a big group of parishes called a diocese. He looks after all the priests and people who live there.

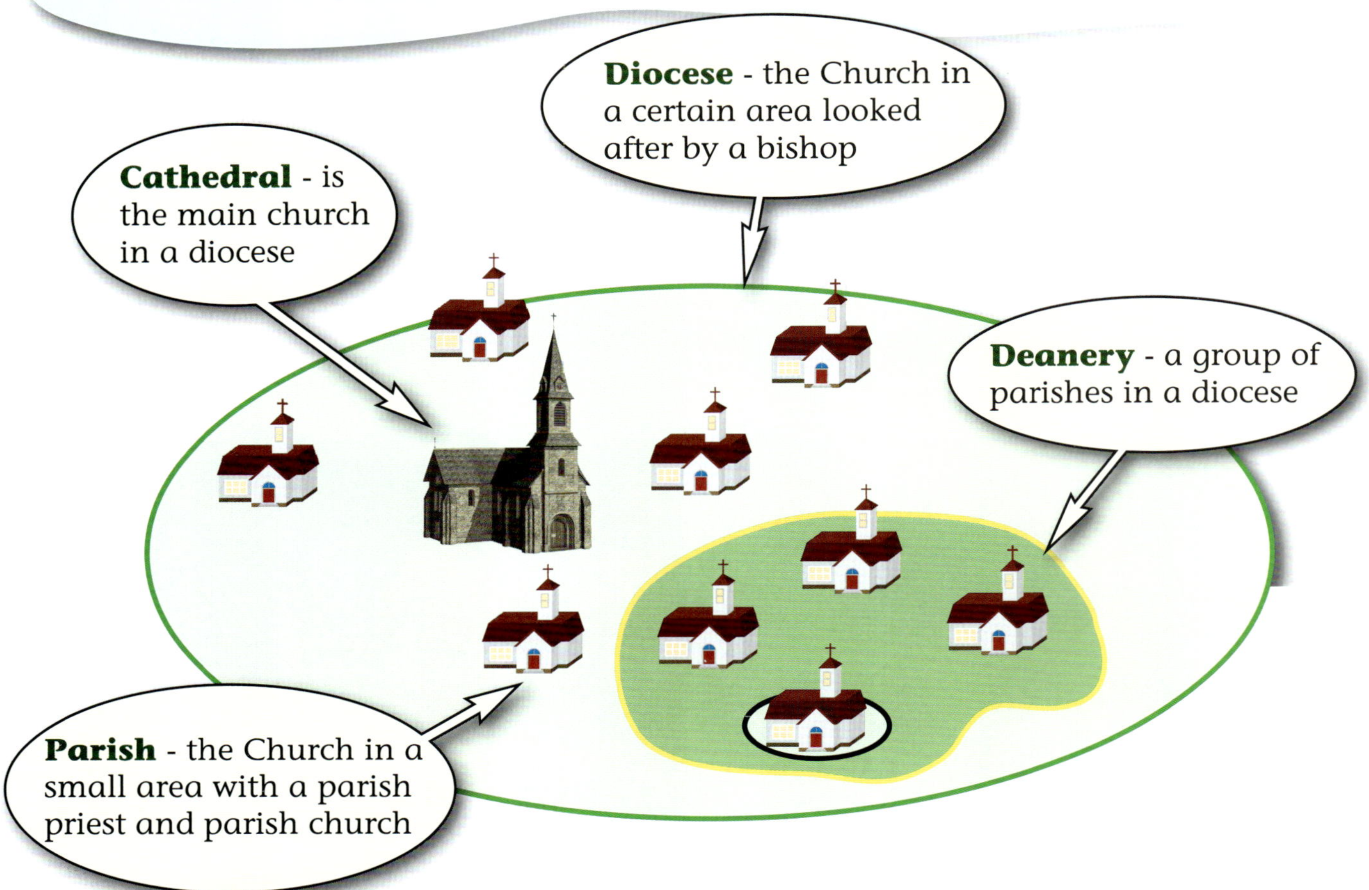

Activities

1. What do you think this image represents? Why?

2. a) The word 'church' has two meanings. Explain what they are?

   b) Could we do without one of them? Why? Why not?

Our Parish Family

We meet with our parish family each week when we go to Mass and at special times throughout the year, such as Easter and Christmas. We also come together with our parish family to celebrate important moments in our lives, for example, when someone is baptised or gets married.

Our parish church is a special building. This is where all the people who live in our parish can come together so that we can praise and thank God as part of His family.

Activities

1. a) What is the name of your parish priest?
   b) What is the name of your parish?
   c) Which diocese are you in?
   d) What is the name of your Bishop?
   e) What is the Pope's name?

2. Work in pairs.
   a) Write a list of questions that you would like to ask your parish priest about his ministry (or work).
   b) Share with the rest of the class.
   c) Choose the ten best questions to send to your priest.

3. Zita

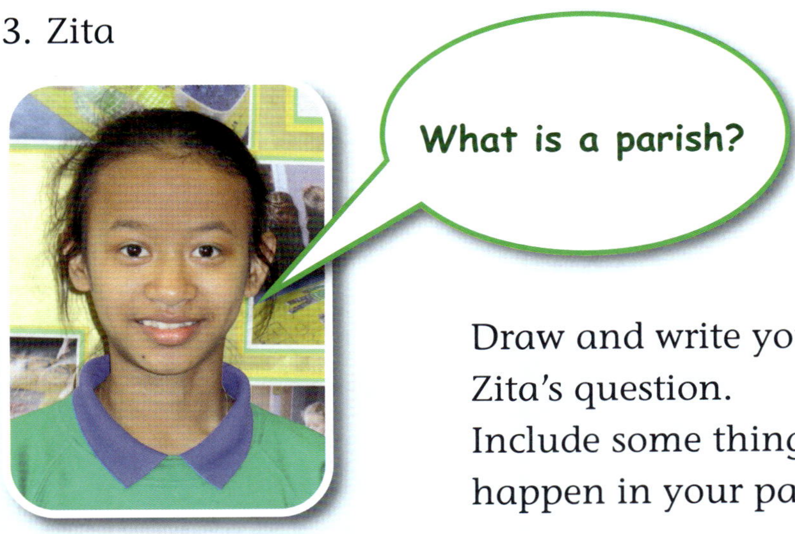

Draw and write your answer to Zita's question.
Include some things that happen in your parish.

Joining the Family of the Church

Know that we join the Church when we receive the Sacrament of Baptism.
Think about what this Sacrament does for us.

The Sacrament of Baptism

A sacrament is a special meeting with Jesus.

In the Sacrament of Baptism we enter into the life of Jesus and receive his Spirit. We become members of the Church and Jesus helps us to live a good life.

Our Baptism

We became members of the Church when we were **baptised**. For most of us, this was when we were little babies. Our parents wanted us to be baptised because they wanted us to grow up in the Church. They also wanted us to live our lives as Jesus showed us.

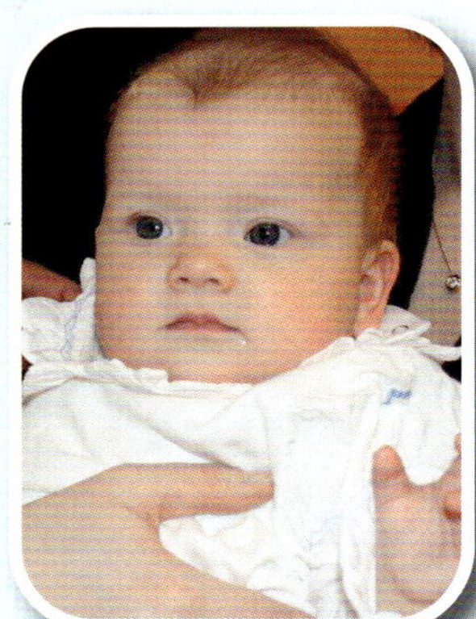

On the day that we were baptised, the priest called us by our own special name. This is our Christian name because when we were baptised we became Christians, followers of Jesus and we joined the Christian family.

What does being a Christian mean?

Being a Christian means that we should try to live our lives in a Christian way, just as Jesus taught us to when he was on earth. He was loving and kind to everyone he met, even to his enemies. He was always willing to forgive people when they did something wrong.

As baptised Christians, we should try to be like Jesus and show love and kindness to all the people we meet, even to those who are unkind to us.

Activities

1. In our Christian family are people who want to live like Jesus lived. What do you think 'living like Jesus' means?

2. a) Write down the names of three people you will meet today.

   b) Next to each name, write down some ways you could show kindness to them.

3. Find out why your name was chosen for you.

Key Words

oil of catechumens   anointed
oil of chrism   godparents

The Sacrament of Baptism

Understand what happens when we receive the Sacrament of Baptism.
Reflect on the meaning of the Sacrament of Baptism.

What happens when we receive the Sacrament of Baptism?

When we are baptised, we enter into the life of Jesus. It is as if we are born again into the life of God.

The parents bring the baby to church to receive the Sacrament of Baptism.

The priest welcomes the family and makes the sign of the cross on the forehead of the baby.

The baby is blessed or anointed with special oil called the oil of catechumens.

The parents and godparents make baptismal promises that they will bring up the baby as a child of God.

Water that has been blessed is poured over the baby's head three times as the priest says, "I baptise you in the name of the Father and of the Son and of the Holy Spirit."

After this, the baby is anointed again with the special oil which is called the oil of chrism.

A white garment is wrapped around the baby. A candle is given to one of the godparents. This is a reminder to the parents that their baby is always to walk in the light of Jesus.

From then on, the baby is a Christian and a member of the Christian family, the Church.

Activities

1. Your teacher will give you details of what happens at a baptism.
   Complete the task on the sheet.

2. Write a prayer to thank God for the day you received the Sacrament of Baptism. Include in your prayer all the people you think were present that day.

3. Research: find out as much as you can about your own baptism.
   Complete the baptism record sheet that your teacher will give you.

4. Plan and role-play a baptism.

Signs and Symbols used in Baptism

Know about some of the signs and symbols used in the Sacrament of Baptism. Reflect on why they are used.

Signs

Signs tell us something in a clear, understandable way. If you look around your classroom or your school, you can probably find lots of different signs.

Activities

a) What does each of the signs above tell us?

b) In what way does each one of them help us?

c) Draw one of the signs in school. Why is it there?

Symbols

A symbol is a different kind of sign. It has many meanings. For example, a gift of flowers can be a is a sign that the person wants to say:

- Thank you;
- Happy Birthday; or
- Sorry.

Activities

Look at these symbols.
Think of at least two meanings for each of them.

Signs and Symbols in Baptism

The signs used in baptism tell us important things as well as showing what is happening. These signs really do make things happen.

Water

Water is a sign of life - without it we could not live. When water is poured over the baby in baptism, it is a sign that the baby is sharing in the new life of Jesus. But the water of Baptism is more than just a sign - it is a sacramental sign. So when we see the water being poured, we know that God is working through it to give the baby new life with Him.

Sign of the Cross

The Sign of the Cross is an important sign for Christians because Jesus died on the cross and rose again after three days. The Sign of the Cross is made on the child's forehead to show that the baby is now part of the Christian family.

Candle

Jesus is the Light of the World. The baptismal candle is a symbol that the light of Jesus has entered the baby's life. This candle is lit from the Easter or Paschal candle on the altar.

White Garment

This is usually a white shawl and is wrapped around the baby towards the end of the baptism. The shawl is put on the baby as a sign that the baby has 'put on' Jesus. This means that the baby shares in the new life of Jesus.

Oil

A special oil that has been blessed by the bishop, is put on the baby's head. This is a sign of the presence of the Holy Spirit who will help the baby in his or her Christian life.

Activities

1. Use the worksheet 'Signs and Symbols at Baptism' that your teacher will give you. Beside each picture, write a sentence explaining what is happening.

2. How do you think the Sacrament of Baptism will help you as you get older?

Promises made at Baptism

Know about the promises made at Baptism by parents and godparents.
Think about the importance of keeping promises.

A Broken Promise?

It was Sita's birthday and she was having a big party with lots of friends. She had been looking forward to it for ages, especially when she heard that her best friend Jenny was coming too!

Sita and Jenny used to go to the same school together but then Jenny's family had moved out of the area and they didn't see each other very often.

Jenny had telephoned Sita during the week. "Yes of course I'm coming," she had said. "I promise! I can't wait to see you again!"

But now, it was the day of the party. Everyone was there except for Jenny. Sita knew she should be joining in the fun and enjoying herself but it just wasn't the same without Jenny. She felt so disappointed - how could Jenny have broken her promise?

Suddenly, the phone rang and Sita was delighted to hear Jenny's voice. "Oh Sita, I'm so sorry. Mum's car broke down. But don't worry, I'll be there soon. I promised, didn't I?" She kept her promise and arrived.

We all know how important promises are and how important it is to keep them. Promises are very important in Baptism too.

Activities

a) How did Sita feel when Jenny promised to come to her party?

b) How did she feel when she thought Jenny had broken that promise?

c) Can you think of an important promise that someone made to you?

d) Did they keep their promise? How did this make you feel?

e) Why do you think a promise made, should be kept and not broken?

Baptismal Promises

On the day that you were baptised, your parents and godparents made very special promises before God. They promised that they believed in God, our Father, in Jesus Christ his Son and in the Holy Spirit. They promised to bring you up as a member of the Catholic Church. Also, they promised to be a good example to you of how a Catholic should live.

Your parents chose two or more people to be your godparents. Your godparents were probably very good friends of your parents or even members of your family. They had to choose your godparents very carefully. This was because they needed good people to help them in their task of bringing you up as a member of God's Christian family.

Activities

1. Imagine you are a parent choosing a godparent for your child.
   a) What sort of person would you want?

   b) What important qualities should she or he have?

2. Research: Find out the names of your godparents.

   a) Ask your parents why they chose them.

   b) If possible, talk to your godparents and find out about their memories of your special day. How did they feel to be chosen as your godparents?

3. Read the **Rite of Baptism** text that your teacher will give you.
   a) What do you think is the most important thing that the priest is saying to the parents.

   b) Why is it important?

   c) What do godparents have to do?

4. Imagine someone you know is going to have their baby baptised soon. Design and make a baptism card that you could give them on their special day. Decorate it with suitable symbols.

2. Mary, Mother of God

**Know that God chose Mary to be the mother of His Son.
Think about the importance of being chosen.**

Being Chosen

Ben was excited. Today, Mrs Barnes the Head Teacher introduced him to the new boy, Mario, from Italy. Ben was asked to look after him for a whole week. Mario had just started learning English, so Ben had to make sure he understood where to go and what to do. He was also responsible for helping him to get to know the other pupils.

All week, Ben worked hard and kept his promise to Mrs Barnes. He got to school a bit early to show Mario where the school hall and sports room were. He went with him into the playground and they played with his best friends, Daniel and Mike. When school finished, he made sure Mario knew what to do for homework. He stayed with him until his Mum came to pick him up. By the end of the week, Ben and Mario had become great friends.

Pause to reflect

- Why do you think Ben was chosen?
- Think of a time when you were chosen to help.
- How did you feel?
- Know that God has chosen each one of us. Think of how special you are to Him.

The Annunciation

God chooses Mary

In the Bible, we can read about a time when God was looking for someone really special to be the Mother of His Son, Jesus. It had to be someone who was kind and good and who would love His Son very much.

One day, God sent the angel Gabriel to see a young girl called Mary who lived in Nazareth. Mary loved God very much, so she listened carefully to what angel Gabriel had to say.

'Hail Mary!' said the angel. **'The Lord is with you.'**
Mary was very surprised to be spoken to in this way, but the angel said,

'Do not be afraid Mary for I bring you good news.'

The angel explained to Mary that God had chosen her to be the mother of a baby boy and that the baby would be called Jesus. He told Mary that this baby would be very special and holy because he would be God's Son. The angel also said that Mary's cousin Elizabeth was going to have a baby even though she was very old, because with God, nothing is impossible!

Mary was amazed to hear all this. She knew that God loved her and she wanted to do whatever He asked. She told the angel that she was ready for whatever God wanted. Then, the angel left. (Luke 1:26-28 adapted)

Although Mary was just an ordinary young girl in lots of ways, God knew that she loved Him very much. He knew that she would love and care for Jesus. Mary put complete trust in God.

Activities

1. In pairs: role-play the visit of the angel to Mary.

2. Write a diary entry for Mary. Mention:
   - the visit from the angel;
   - the good news;
   - how she felt;
   - the answer she gave to the angel and the reason for it.

3. a) Choose one of the pictures of the Annunciation on this page.

   b) Describe what is similar and what is different from the picture on page 21.

   c) Which one do you prefer? Why?

Mary visits Elizabeth

**Know that Mary went to visit her cousin Elizabeth.
Think about how we can help each other.**

Sharing Good News

Olivia's dad was in the army and she had not seen him for a few months. One evening after school, her mum was waiting with a very big smile on her face, she had great news! Dad was coming home and would be with them in a few days.

Olivia could not wait to tell her friends the next day. Everybody was happy for her. Immediately, she started thinking about how good it would be to have him at home.

Pause to share your 'Good News'.

Mary goes to see Elizabeth

Mary wanted to share her good news and help her cousin Elizabeth.

Soon after the angel told Mary that she would be the Mother of Jesus, Mary got ready and hurried off to a town in the hill country of Judea. She went to visit her cousin Elizabeth who lived with her husband Zechariah.

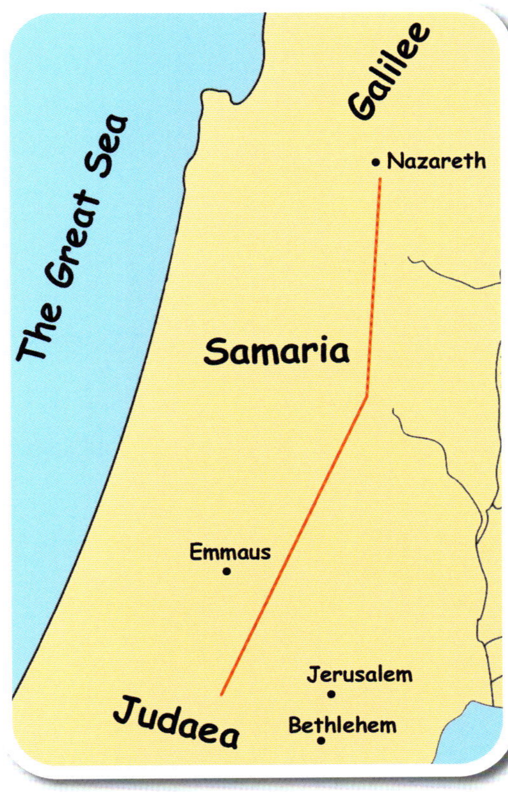

Nazareth to Judea is about 80 miles.

Mary greeted Elizabeth. Straight away, Elizabeth knew through the Holy Spirit that Mary was going to have a baby, a very special baby, the Son of God. She said, "Mary, you are the most holy of all women and the child you will have is most holy! How is it that the woman who is going to have God's Son should come and visit me?" (Luke 1:39-45 adapted)

Mary spoke words of praise and love for God. She stayed with Elizabeth for three months and then she went home to Nazareth.

Did you know?

The Hail Mary is based on the words of the angel Gabriel and the words of Elizabeth when Mary went to visit her.

These words remind us that Mary was 'blessed' because she believed in the word of God; so the child that Mary gave birth to was the Son of God, who would grow up to become the saviour of the world.

"Hail Mary, full of grace,
the Lord is with you.
Blessed are you among women
and blessed is the fruit of your womb, Jesus."

The Church has added the second part:

"Holy Mary, Mother of God,
pray for us sinners,
now and at the hour of our death. Amen."

Activities

1. Zechariah, Elizabeth's husband, was not there when Mary arrived.
   What do you think Elizabeth told him when he came home?

2. Give examples of how:
   a) Mary trusted in God.

   b) Elizabeth trusted in God.

   c) You trust in God.

3. Mary made a long journey to help Elizabeth.
   a) What do you think she was able to do for her?

   b) God asks us to love and help each other.
   What are the most important things you can do to help:
   - at home;
   - at school?

4. Mary visited Elizabeth to share her 'Good News'.
   a) What was it?

   b) How is Mary's 'Good News', good news for us?

Key Words

annunciation angel Gabriel
swaddling clothes Jews Christ
wise men worship Saviour Lord

Mystery of the Incarnation

Know about the Mystery of the Incarnation.
Reflect on mysteries.

Mysteries

Sometimes, we struggle to find answers to questions. This may be because we need to study a lot to find out. But there are other types of questions that are very difficult because no one really knows the answer. These questions are called **mysteries**.

God wants us to think about these mysteries even though we cannot fully understand them. For example, God is a very great mystery. We will never fully understand Him but He has made Himself known to us in a wonderful way.

We are now going to explore this mystery.

The Mystery of the Incarnation

The mystery of the Incarnation means that God became a **real human being**. He was born as a little baby. Mary was his mother.

God was a real human baby called Jesus. He grew up to be a boy like other boys and then a man. As a child, he lived with Mary and his foster father, Joseph, in Nazareth.

The BIG mystery is that at the same time Jesus is truly God.

Think of the things he did that no man could do. He had power over the wind and the sea, he could cure the sick and work many other miracles.

The mystery of God becoming human is too big for us to understand but we believe it, because God told us. So we believe that God has come to earth in human form and his name is Jesus.

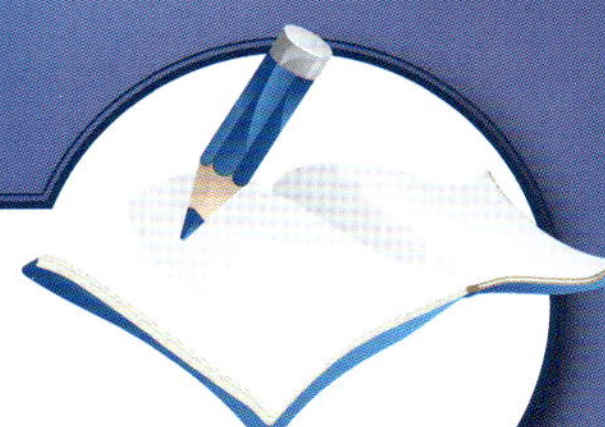

Activities

a) Think of what you know about Jesus which shows that he is:
   - truly God;
   - truly human.

b) Draw two boxes in your book and give examples.

I think Jesus is truly human because...	I think Jesus is truly God because...

Why did God come to earth?

From the very beginning, God gave his people the gift of freedom to choose between good and evil. It was a very important gift because he wanted us to be free to love Him - or not to love Him.

We see in the story of Adam and Eve that people chose to do evil rather than good. But God didn't give up on them. Again and again, He sent holy men, like Moses and the prophets, to tell His people how they should live, but they still ignored Him.

So, in the end, God sent Jesus to save us from sin and death - which is the result of sin. **If we believe in Jesus, we will have eternal life with him in heaven.** God became man so that everyone could look at Jesus' life and see what it really means to love God. Knowing Jesus, we know what true love is.

Activities

1. a) In groups, think of all the questions you would like to ask Jesus.
   b) Share your questions with the rest of the class.
   c) Try to answer the ones that are not mysteries.

2. Think of what you know about Jesus.
   How does he show what true love is?

3. Imagine your grandmother wants to know what you have been learning in school.
   What you would tell her about the mystery of the Incarnation?

Advent

Understand that Advent is a time to prepare to celebrate the birth of Jesus.
Think about how we can prepare.

What does Advent mean?

The four weeks leading up to Christmas are an important time for us. We call this time Advent. During Advent, we prepare to celebrate the birth of Jesus.

The word Advent means 'coming' and during Advent we think especially about the coming of Jesus at Christmas! This can be a very exciting time as we rush around wrapping Christmas presents, writing Christmas cards, decorating trees with lights and tinsel. But it is very important that we remember what we are really preparing for, the birth of Jesus.

There are lots of ways we can remind ourselves during Advent of the great event that will happen on Christmas Day.

Advent Wreath

The Advent wreath has four candles, one for each week of Advent. Some wreaths have a white candle in the middle to be lit on Christmas Day. The wreath is made of evergreen and is in the shape of a circle, with no beginning or end, to remind us of God's never-ending love for us. By lighting the candles on the Advent wreath and saying Advent prayers, we remember that we are waiting for Jesus to come at Christmas.

Activities

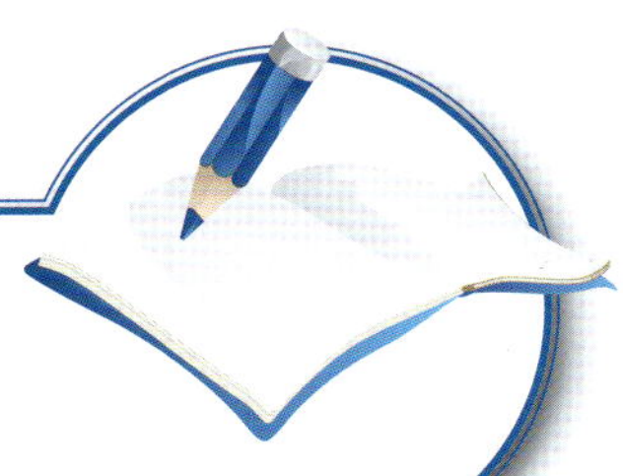

1. a) Why is the Advent wreath always a circle?
   b) Why are there four candles?

2. a) Work in pairs to write an Advent prayer.
   b) Share your prayer with the rest of the class.

Advent Promises

Another way we can prepare to celebrate the birth of Jesus is to make an Advent Promise. This can be something very simple like setting aside a little time every day to talk and pray to Jesus; or promising to be extra helpful at home. You don't have to tell anyone your promise – it is between you and God!

Activities

1. Make an Advent Promise!
   a) Spend some time thinking about what this might be.
   b) Draw a wreath and write your promise in the middle of it. Place it in your class prayer corner.
2. Write a letter to Jesus! Tell him why you are looking forward to his birthday. Ask for something really special that would bring happiness to others.

Christmas Crib

Every church and lots of homes have cribs during Advent.

When we look at a crib, we remember where and how Jesus was born. In some cribs the manger is left empty until Christmas Day when the figure of baby Jesus is added.

Activity

Prepare a liturgy for blessing the Crib.

- Choose a Christmas carol.
- Write some bidding prayers.

Christmas Cards

Sending Christmas cards is a lovely way to remind people that we are waiting for Jesus to be born. However, be careful! Some Christmas cards have nothing to do with the real meaning of Christmas.

Have a good look at the Christmas cards you receive this year. Sort them into two piles – ones that show that we are waiting for the coming of Jesus and ones which don't! Take time to reflect on them.

Activities

1. Do you think Christmas cards are important? Give reasons for your answer.

2. Design a Christmas card that you could send to a friend. Make sure your card shows what Christmas is really about!

3. a) Look at catalogues advertising Christmas cards.
   b) Choose one catalogue that has very few or no cards which show the real meaning of Christmas.
   c) Write a letter to the catalogue company. Explain why it is important to include cards which show the real meaning of Christmas.

Dear

My name is

My schools is

Many of your cards

I would like to see more cards

The reasons for this are

With best wishes

The Birth of Jesus

Know about the birth of Jesus.
Reflect on what this means for us.

Journey to Bethlehem

Just before Jesus was born, Mary and Joseph had to make a long journey. This time they had to go all the way to Bethlehem!

This would have been a difficult journey in those days when there were no trains, buses or cars! When Mary and Joseph arrived in Bethlehem the town was so busy that there was no room in any of the inns and nowhere for them to stay.

Mary must have felt very tired and weary by this time. So, when they were offered a stable for the night, she was delighted.

Pause to reflect

- Think of the long journey Mary and Joseph had to make.
- There were no telephones or Internet to make a booking in an inn.
- There were no cars or trains for a comfortable journey.
- Even though it was difficult, God was with them and they trusted in Him.

Jesus is Born

These days when a woman is having a baby, there is a long list of things that have to be bought – a cot, blankets, nappies, toys! But Mary had none of these for her child.

The Bible tells us that while Mary and Joseph were in Bethlehem, the time came for Mary to have her baby.

"And she gave birth to her firstborn son and wrapped him in swaddling clothes, and laid him in a manger, because there was no place for them in the inn" (Luke 2:7-8).

How simple this sounds and yet, of all the babies ever born, this baby was the most special. This was God, God who had come down to earth in the form of a little baby to be our Saviour.

Activities

1. a) Make a list of the best ways to prepare for Christmas.
   b) Underline the three most important ways for you.
   c) Say why you have chosen these three ways.

2. Imagine some of your friends who are not Christians want to know why Christmas is so important for us.
   Role-play the conversation with the person next to you.

The Shepherds

At that time Jesus was born, another extraordinary event took place.
"In that region there were shepherds out in the field, keeping watch over their flock by night. And the angel of the Lord appeared to them, and the glory of the Lord shone around them, and they were filled with fear.

Then, the angel said to them, 'Be not afraid; for behold I bring you good news of great joy which will come to all the people; for to you is born this day in the city of David, a Saviour who is Christ the Lord. And this will be a sign for you: you will find the babe wrapped in swaddling clothes and lying in a manger'" (Luke 2:6-11).

Can you imagine how the shepherds felt? They were amazed! For a few minutes, they did not know what was happening. They had never seen angels before and they knew this was an extraordinary event.

The message of the angels was very strange; they just had to find out for themselves.

They left their sheep and hurried down the hillside. They found Mary, Joseph and the baby Jesus.

Immediately, when they saw Jesus, they knelt down and worshipped him. They remembered what the angels said to them and they believed that Jesus would be the Saviour of the world.

Mary and Joseph were very puzzled by the visit of the shepherds. So the shepherds told them what had happened and the message that the angels had given to them.

Activities

1. Imagine you are Mary being interviewed in Bethlehem. Write your answers to the following questions:
   a) What is so special about your baby?

   b) What do you think about everything that has happened to you?

   c) How did the shepherds know where to find you?

2. The shepherds hurried away and told their neighbours and friends the exciting news.
   a) What do you think they said?

   b) What was most important about it?

   c) How is that important for us now?

3. Why do you think God chose shepherds to be the first to receive the 'Good News'?

Visit of the Wise Men

Know that Wise Men came to worship Jesus.
Think about the gifts we can offer to Jesus.

The Wise Men

When Jesus was born in Bethlehem, he received a visit from some wise men. First, they went to see King Herod and asked him, "Where is he who has been born king of the Jews? For we have seen his star in the East, and have come to worship him" (Matthew 2:2).

King Herod was jealous – he didn't want anyone else to be king but himself! So, he said to the wise men, "Go and find this baby and when you have found him, come back and tell me where he is so that I can worship him myself". Herod really wanted to kill the baby Jesus.

The wise men left Herod and continued to follow the star until it stopped over the place where Jesus was with Mary and Joseph.

"When they saw the child and Mary, his mother, they fell down and worshipped him. Then, opening their treasures, they offered him gifts of gold, frankincense and myrrh. And being warned in a dream not to return to Herod, they departed to their own country by another way" (Matthew. 2:8-10).

The Gifts

By giving Jesus **gold**, the wise men were saying that they wanted Jesus to be King and Lord of their lives. The gift of **frankincense** was a sign that they wanted to worship Jesus as the true God. The gift of **myrrh** was a symbol of sorrow. With the gift of myrrh, a perfume used for the dead, the wise men were saying that Jesus had come to die to forgive our sins and lead us to God.

Activities

1. a) How did the wise men know where to find Jesus?

   b) Why do you think the wise men knelt down before a little baby?

2. **Hot Seating:** The three wise men are in the 'hot seats' and the rest of the class ask them questions. Think about:
   - How did they know about Jesus?
   - How did they find the way?
   - Why did they go to Herod?
   - Why did they choose to bring gold, frankincense and myrrh?
   - When would their gifts be useful for Jesus?
   - Were they going to go back to Herod? Why? Why not?

3. Soon, we will be celebrating the birth of Jesus.
   Think carefully about the gifts you would like to offer him.
   Draw two gift boxes and write the contents on the outside.

3. Sacrament of Reconciliation

Understand what it means to make wrong choices.
Reflect on how wrong choices affect us and other people.

The Great Commandment

No matter where we go we find there are rules. Some are hard to follow. Some we don't like. However, we know they are there to help us and keep us safe.

Pause to discuss

- What are the rules in school?
- Are they good? Why?
- In what ways are these rules intended to help us and keep us safe?
- Think about the rules at home?
- How do they help you and other members of the family?

Jesus gave us one BIG rule. It is called the **Great Commandment** and has two parts to it:

Love God with all your Heart
and
Your Neighbour as Yourself.

Pause to reflect

- Why do you think Jesus gave us this rule?
- How do you think it will help us?
- Is it difficult to keep it? Why? Why not?

Activity

In what ways does the Great Commandment help us and keep us safe? Think about how love affects everything.

The Great Commandment is not always easy to keep because loving our neighbour means being kind and helpful to **everybody**, not just the people we like.

In the coming weeks, we will learn about the special help Jesus gives us to keep his Great Commandment because sometimes this is difficult and we make wrong choices.

Making Wrong Choices

Have you ever fallen out with a friend? Have you ever quarrelled with someone and afterwards felt really sad and wished you could make things up again?

It happened to a boy called Joe. Read what he wrote in his diary.

Thursday 4th March

Dear Diary
I've had a rotten day today.
It all started at morning play when I was playing football. My best friend Steve kicked my football over the school fence into the road. He said sorry and I know it was an accident but at the time I just felt really angry. I shouted at him and called him stupid and then I said I'd never let him play again.

We didn't talk to each other all day. Now, I just feel really miserable. I wish I could make everything all right again. I didn't mean any of those things I said to Steve. What can I do to make friends with him again? What if he won't forgive me? Is there any way I can put this right?

We have all felt like this at some time or another. We have all hurt friends by saying something or doing something that causes them pain and afterwards wished we could put it right. Well, Jesus tells us we can put it right. He tells us that if we really are sad and sorry for the wrong choices we have made, we can say sorry, ask to be forgiven and try to find a way of making things right again.

Another word for making things right is **'reconciliation'**. When Joe says he wants Steve to forgive him and be his friend again, what he wants is to be **reconciled** with Steve. He wants to put things right between them so that they can both be happy again.

Read what happened to Joe and Steve the next day.

Friday 5th March

Dear Diary
Today was much better! Everything is sorted out between us; Steve and I are friends again.

I saw him walking ahead of me as we were going to school today. I ran to catch up with him. I was nervous in case he just ignored me or wouldn't talk to me. I said I was sorry for yesterday and that I didn't mean what I said. Steve was really good about it. He could have just refused to talk to me but he forgave me. And the best thing was, when we got to school, there was the football in the middle of the school playground. Someone must have found it in the road and thrown it back over the fence!

Joe felt sorry for what he had done, he told his friend he was sorry and he tried to put things right. His friend forgave him.

Activities

1. Steve forgave Joe for being mean to him.
   What does this tell you about Steve?

2. a) What do you think Jesus would say if you argued with someone?
   b) Why do you think he would say this?

3. Can you think of a time when you argued with a friend?
   Write your own diary entry about what happened.
   Make sure you include how you were both reconciled.

4. Do you think it is easy to forgive someone who has hurt you?
   Explain your answer.

Called to Change

Know how Jesus called people to turn away from sin. Think about why this is important.

What is Sin?

Sin is when we fail to love God and others. It is when we choose to do something hurtful to another person. It is when we deliberately choose to do something that we know is wrong. For example, it is when we tell a lie.

Pause to discuss:

a) Why wasn't the broken window an accident?
b) Why do you think the boy chose to tell a lie?
c) What might have happened if he had owned up?
d) What will be the consequences of his lie?

God's Love

God is waiting to help us. We know, for certain, that God will always forgive us if we are sorry for our sins. We can say 'sorry' to God at any time. When something bad happens that is not our fault, it is **not** a sin.

Activities

1. Look at these two examples.
   For each one, explain why it **was** or **was not** a sin.

   a) Sophie's mum left a precious vase on the table. Sophie was clearing the table, knocked over the vase, it landed on the floor in tiny bits.

   b) John wanted to use the computer but his brother got to it first. John was furious and gave him a very hard punch.

2. In groups, think of two more examples.
   Explain why they **were** or **were not** sins.
   Share with the class.

Zacchaeus meets Jesus

When Jesus lived here on earth, he helped many people to change their lives for the better. He helped them to stop being selfish, because being selfish only made them and other people unhappy. He showed them how they could change and how they could make things right again.

One of the people Jesus helped was a man called Zacchaeus. Zacchaeus was a 'sinner' – he was selfish and did not show love to those around him. He was a tax-collector and was taking more money from people than he should have done.

Zacchaeus had become very rich because he was dishonest and treated people unfairly. He wanted to know about Jesus who was coming to his town. Zacchaeus was short and couldn't see anything over the heads of the crowd.

So Zacchaeus climbed a tree to get a better view.

As Jesus passed, he saw him up in the tree and said, "Come down Zacchaeus. I want to stay in your house tonight."

Zacchaeus was amazed that Jesus should choose to eat in his house because he was a sinner! Quickly, he slid down the tree, took Jesus home and they had a wonderful meal together.

But some people in the crowd were very angry about this. They could not understand why Jesus would choose to be friends with a sinner. Zacchaeus, on the other hand, was very happy. He knew there was something amazing about Jesus, something that made him want to change and become a better person.

There and then, he decided that he would not cheat people any more. He was sorry that he had ever done so. To make things right, he promised to pay back all the money he had made by cheating people. Also, he decided to give a lot of money to the poor.

Zacchaeus changed when he met Jesus. He no longer sinned. Instead of thinking just about himself, he thought of other people and how he could help them.

Activities

1. Discuss: why would a sinner like Zacchaeus want to see Jesus?
2. In small groups: imagine you are part of the crowd. How did you feel when you saw Jesus going to Zacchaeus' house?
3. What do you think Jesus said to help Zacchaeus become a good person?
4. After meeting with Jesus, Zacchaeus' life changed for the better. How?
5. Choose one part of the story of Zacchaeus. Write a play-script for it.

God's Love

Understand that God always loves us.
Think of how important this love is for us.

God will never forget about us

When he was on earth, Jesus met many people who were sinners. He called them to change their ways and become better people. He told them that God loved them very much and wanted to forgive them. Here is one story Jesus told. It touched the hearts of many people he met.

The Lost Sheep

There was once a shepherd who had many sheep in his flock. He loved them very much and took great care of all of them.

However, one day, when he was counting his sheep, one of them was missing. So he left his flock in the field and went off and searched all day for the one sheep that was lost.

At last, as night began to fall, the shepherd found the lost sheep alone, frightened and shivering.

He was delighted. Straight away, he picked up the little sheep and carried it on his shoulders back to the flock. That night, he called his friends and family together and said, “Let’s celebrate because I have found the sheep which was lost!” (Luke 15:4-7 adapted)

Jesus told this story because the shepherd is a bit like God. God loves us all very much just as the shepherd loved his flock of sheep. Sometimes, we get ‘lost’ – we do selfish or thoughtless things and we feel far away from God - but, like the shepherd, God will help us to come back to Him. He is in love with us and will never, ever forget us. He is always thinking of us. Even if we have done wrong, He will never turn away from us. He is there waiting for us to turn back to Him.

Activities

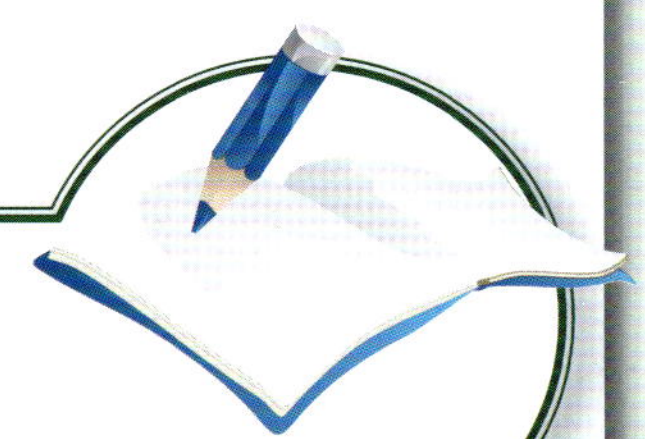

1. Discuss the story ‘The Lost Sheep’.
   What does it tell us about God?

2. Sometimes we get ‘lost’. Give examples to explain what this means.

3. Imagine you are the lost sheep.
   Write a letter of thanks to the shepherd.

4. Design a poster with the caption, ‘God is my Shepherd’.
   Think about how you will illustrate your poster.

5. Alex has had a bad day. He has upset his mum and dad.
   Now, he thinks God is angry with him.
   What would you say to Alex to help him understand why God is not angry with him?

The Sacrament of Reconciliation

Know what the Sacrament of Reconciliation means.
Reflect on God's love and forgiveness.

God will always love us

The Bible tells us just how much God loves us even when we sin and turn away from Him.

God says:

I have loved you ever since you were a child.
Even though you may have turned away from me,
I called you back.
It was I who taught you to walk.
I held you in my arms
even though you did not recognise me.
I was always with you.
I have always loved you (Hosea 11:1-3).

Pause to reflect

- Think of the tremendous love God has for you.
- Take time to be with Him and to say 'Thank You'.
- Tell Him how much you love Him.

God's Forgiveness

There are times when we need God's forgiveness. Sometimes, we make choices that hurt others and we fail to love as God has asked us. God still loves us very much, He will never stop loving us. However, we feel unhappy about some of the things we have said or done. We fail to love others as God has asked, so we want to make things right with God and others.

The Sacrament of Reconciliation is a chance for us to do just this. It is a chance for us to say sorry, and to start again.

Activities

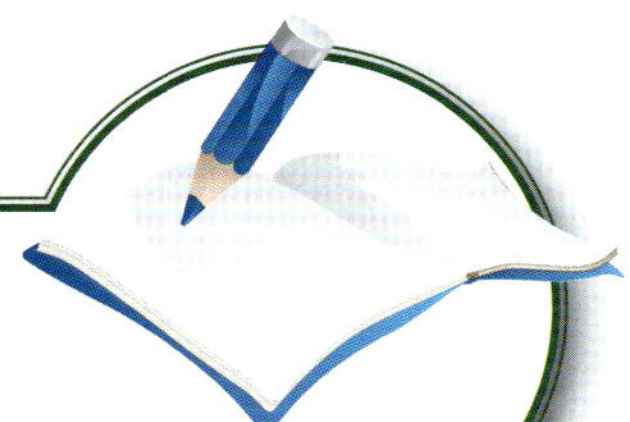

1. Study the picture illustrating God's forgiveness.
   a) What do you think the artist wants us to
      - feel?
      - understand?
      - do?

   b) Draw your own picture illustrating forgiveness and write an explanation for it.

2. a) Choose your favourite lines from the writing of Hosea. Write them out and illustrate them.

   b) What do these words tell you about God's love for you?

The Sacrament of Reconciliation

When we receive the Sacrament of Reconciliation, we can be certain that because God loves us so much, He forgives us for all the wrong things we have done.

We often call the Sacrament of Reconciliation 'Confession'. So every time we go to confession, God offers us a special grace to help us to love others and grow very close to Him.

Even when we have no big sins to confess, we need to remember the little things we have done which upset other people. We should try to go to confession regularly because when we do, we receive an abundance of God's great love for us!

Activities

1. Look carefully at this picture. Some children are being unkind and hurtful.

   a) Make a list of some of the wrong things you can see.

   b) Imagine you are the teacher for those pupils. What would you say to them when they went back to class?

   c) Why do you think some of the children in the picture might want to receive the Sacrament of Reconciliation?

2. Study the worksheet 'My Conscience' your teacher will give you. Complete the tasks.

Receiving the Sacrament of Reconciliation

Know what happens during the Sacrament of Reconciliation. Think about what this Sacrament does for us.

My conscience

When I am trying to decide if what I have done is right or wrong, I use my conscience. Conscience is that feeling inside that tells me what is right and what is wrong. It is like God's little bell.

I have a duty to inform my conscience so that I make the right decisions. I inform my conscience by listening to Jesus and what the Church teaches. I also inform my conscience by listening to the advice of those who have a responsibility for me, for example, my parents or teachers.

In preparation for Confession I examine my conscience.

Pause

Work in pairs. Make a list of questions you could ask yourself when examining your conscience.

What happens when I go to confession?

The Sacrament of Reconciliation is much more than confessing sins, it is more about receiving God's great love and mercy.

In **Confession**, the priest is there to help us. He represents God and through him we receive God's forgiveness.

When we have made our confession, the priest will ask us to say a prayer or do something to show that we are truly sorry and want to put things right. This is called a **penance**.

We know for certain that the priest will **never** repeat anything told in Confession.

Before Confession

1. I think about what I have done to hurt other people. Have I been unkind or selfish?

2. I pray for the grace to be truly sorry for my sins.

3. I tell God that I want to change and turn back to Him.

At Confession

1. I tell the priest how long it is since my last Confession.

2. I tell him the things I have done wrong on purpose.

3. The priest will give me a penance.

4. I tell God I am really sorry by saying an 'Act of Contrition'.

5. God forgives me through the words of the priest.

6. I say 'thank you' to the priest.

An Act of Contrition (Sorrow)

O my God, because you are so good,
I am very sorry that I have sinned against you,
and with the help of your grace,
I will try not to sin again.

After Confession

1. I say my penance, or think about what the priest has asked me to do.

2. I thank God for His forgiveness and love.

Activities

1. Learn the 'Act of Contrition' by heart.
   When you think you know it, test each other.

2. What do you think is best about receiving the Sacrament of Reconciliation? Think of at least two things.

3. Make a pocket sized guide for yourself: 'How to go to Confession'.
   Include what you should do:
   - before Confession;
   - at Confession;
   - after Confession.

4. Why should we try to go to Confession regularly even if we have done only little things that are wrong?

4. Celebrating the Mass

Know what happened at the Last Supper.
Reflect on how the Mass makes this real for us.

The Big Day

The children in St. Ignatius Church in Tokyo, Japan, had been preparing for many months for their First Holy Communion. They started by exploring how the Mass began, so we will do the same.

How did the Mass begin?

What happens at Mass happened at the Last Supper which Jesus shared with his apostles.

Jesus told the apostles that he would have to suffer and die, but that he would rise from the dead. Then, he would go back to his Father and send his Spirit to be with them. They were very puzzled. They didn't know what to say, so they waited to see what would happen.

It was the feast of the Jewish Passover. Jesus was a Jew so he wanted to celebrate this important feast with his very close friends, the apostles.

The Last Supper

This is what happened. Every year, the Jewish people ate a special meal called the Passover meal. Jesus told the apostles that he had been longing to eat this Passover meal with them before he suffered.

So when they were all settled around the table,
"Jesus took some bread, and when he had given thanks, broke it and gave it to them, saying, **'This is my body which is given for you. Do this in remembrance of me'**. Taking the cup, Jesus said: **'This cup which is poured out for you is the new covenant in my blood'"**
(Luke 22:19-20).

Activity

Study the faces of the apostles in the picture above.

a) What questions do you think they want to ask Jesus?
b) How do you think they are feeling?

The Meaning of the Last Supper

Jesus knew that he was going to be betrayed, handed over to his enemies and that he would be put to death on a cross. He freely accepted this suffering and offered his life in love to his Father. This was the most perfect sacrifice which took away the sins committed by everyone, through all ages, right down to you and me and people yet to come.

The Sacrifice of the Mass

By his death on the cross, Jesus shows his great love for his Father and for us. When Jesus died on the cross, he gave everything to God the Father. This is why we call Jesus' death a sacrifice of love. Jesus' love did not die when he died. His love was so perfect it overcame death and he rose triumphantly.

At Mass, we celebrate that Jesus is alive and always with us. His act of self-giving love is made present for us when the bread and wine is changed into his Body and Blood.

This is a mystery – we don't understand how it happens, but we believe that it takes place through the power of the Holy Spirit and the action of the priest at Mass.

We understand that if we are to take an active part in the Mass, we must join Jesus, with all his followers, in offering ourselves in love to the Father and to all people.

Pause to reflect

Close your eyes for two minutes.
Ask Jesus to help you understand his great love for you.

Our Part in the Mass

The reason why we should go to Mass on Sundays and take an active part in it is:

- to be able to offer ourselves in love with Jesus to the Father;
- to receive Jesus in Holy Communion;
- to get the strength to be able to love all our brothers and sisters in the world.

Activities

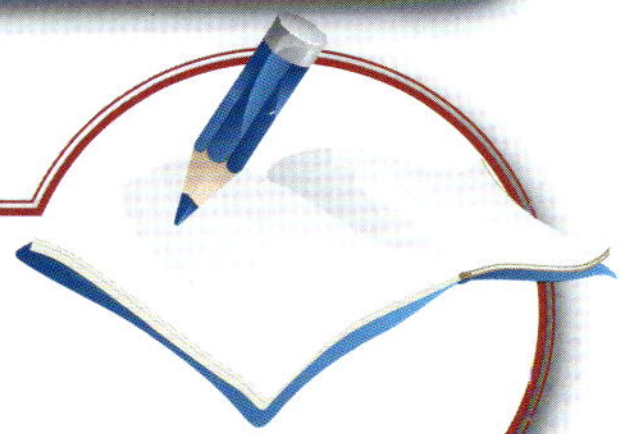

1. a) How is Sunday a special day for you? (For example, time to play with friends, no school.)

   b) Are there any ways you can make Sunday different and show God that you love Him?

2. a) Think about the reasons that pupils have given for going to Mass on Sundays:

   "I go to Mass to talk to Jesus."

   "It makes me feel peaceful to go to Mass."

   "I want to receive Jesus in Holy Communion."

   b) Think of two other reasons and write them down.

The New Covenant

Jesus said: 'This cup which is poured out for you is the **new covenant** in my blood.'

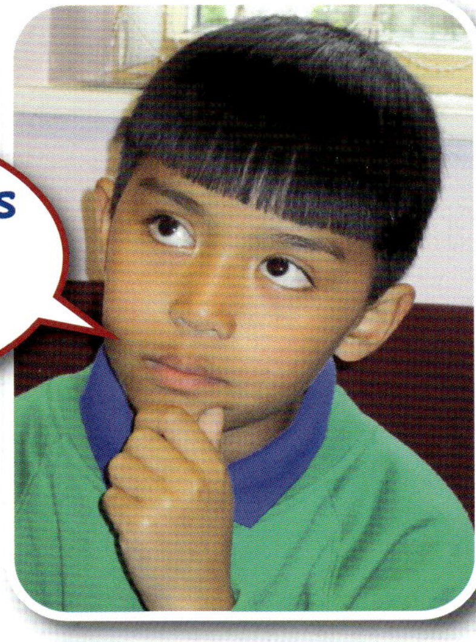

The new covenant is an agreement that Jesus has made with us. Jesus has **handed over** his life in love for us. He opened a **new way** for us to have **a very close friendship** with him. This wonderful new covenant is the promise Jesus made with us. He promises **everlasting happiness** and **life with him in heaven.**

Activities

1. a) Slowly re-read 'The New Covenant'.

   b) Look at the phrases in bold type. Choose one that is important to you. Explain why.

   c) How can we thank Jesus?
   (Clue: Think about the Great Commandment).

2. Draw a circle. Put Jesus in the middle.
   Put thought bubbles around it to indicate what you can do to show your love for Jesus by helping others.
   Make five suggestions.

Get Ready

Your teacher will tell you about a special project to present to your parents at the end of this unit. (Teacher's Book p.65 and p.74)

The Beginning of Mass

Understand what happens at the beginning of Mass.
Think about why we say 'sorry'.

Asking for Forgiveness

At the beginning of Mass, we ask Jesus to forgive us for the wrong choices we have made.

We think of the times when we have said something unkind, or insisted on having our own way and hurt others.

Pause to reflect

- What happens to the friendship we have with another person when we hurt them?
- How do we feel?
- How does the other person feel?
- How can we put things right again?

Saying 'sorry'

Jesus wants us to be kind and helpful to one another. We know what it is like when we are hurt or when we hurt others. Saying 'sorry' takes courage, it's not easy, but at Mass, Jesus will give us help if we ask him.

When we say 'sorry', Jesus is smiling down on us and saying, 'Well done! I am with you!' So, our bond of love and friendship grows stronger.

The Penitential Act

At the beginning of Mass, the priest invites us to think of the times we have failed to be kind and helpful to others. We call this the Penitential Act.

One of the Penitential Acts

Priest: Have mercy on us, O Lord.

People: For we have sinned against you.

Priest: Show us, O Lord, your mercy.

People: And grant us your salvation.

Activities

1. Joe and Steve have been unkind to each other.

   a) What should they do when they go to Mass?

   b) What should they do after Mass?

2. a) How do you think saying 'sorry' helps you?

   b) How do you think it helps the other person?

   c) What is the best thing about saying 'sorry'?

The Readings at Mass

**Understand the importance of the Readings at Mass.
Reflect on how we listen to God's Word.**

God's Word

If we listen carefully, we will find that some of the words have a special message for us. This may be a message to comfort us if we are worried or a few words to help us to live good lives. For example, Jesus said:

"Do not let your hearts be troubled. Trust in God and trust in me" (John 14:1).

"I am the Way, the Truth and the Life" (John 14:6).

"I give you a new commandment: love one another" (John 13:14).

Activity

Which one of these quotations would:

a) help you if you were worried;

b) remind you what to do if you had hurt someone;

c) remind you what to do if someone said they were sorry for hurting you?

Listening to the Readings

When we listen to the Readings from the Bible, we are hearing God's Word. Sometimes, the readings are difficult to understand so we have to listen, not only with our ears, but also with our hearts and minds.

Let's try listening to the reading of the **"Cure of the centurion's servant"** (Matthew 8: 5-10).

Pause and share

What do you think is the most important message in this reading?

Activities

1. Your teacher will give you a copy of the text 'The Cure of the Centurion's servant'.
   a) Read it slowly and then read the explanation.
   b) What does this text tell us about the centurion?
   c) Why do you think Jesus wanted to help the centurion?
   d) What is the most extraordinary thing about this event?
   e) What did Jesus tell the Jews about this centurion?

2. Sometimes, Sarah forgets to listen carefully to the Readings at Mass.
   a) Explain to her why it is important to listen.
   b) Give her some good listening tips.

The Offertory and Consecration

Know what happens at the Offertory and the Consecration.
Think about the offerings we can make.

The Offertory

In the Mass, gifts of bread and wine are taken to the altar. This is because Jesus used bread and wine at the Last Supper. In our hearts, we make an offering to Jesus of ourselves, our good work in school and the help we give at home. Jesus unites our offering to his and offers all to the Father.

Pause to reflect

Think about the gifts you can offer to Jesus.

The Consecration

This is the most important part of the Mass.

The priest speaks the words that Jesus spoke to his apostles at the Last Supper.

Through the power of the Holy Spirit and the action of the priest, Jesus becomes truly present under the form of bread and wine. We still see bread and wine but we believe this is Jesus.

Words of Consecration

Jesus broke the bread, gave it to his disciples and said:

"Take this, all of you, and eat of it,
for this is my Body,
which will be given up for you."

Then, the priest takes the chalice with wine in it and repeats the words of Jesus:

"Take this, all of you, and drink from it,
for this is the chalice of my Blood,
the Blood of the new and eternal covenant,
which will be poured out for you and for many,
for the forgiveness of sins.

Do this in memory of me."

Pause to reflect

This is a very special time in the Mass.

- We try to remember that Jesus is present.
- He wants to be very close to us.
- We listen carefully to the words of the priest.
- We invite Jesus to come to us.

Holy Communion

Know that it is Jesus we receive in Holy Communion. Reflect on this very great gift.

Making Preparations

What do you do when your very best friend is coming to see you? How do you prepare for their visit?

When your friend arrives, what do you do?

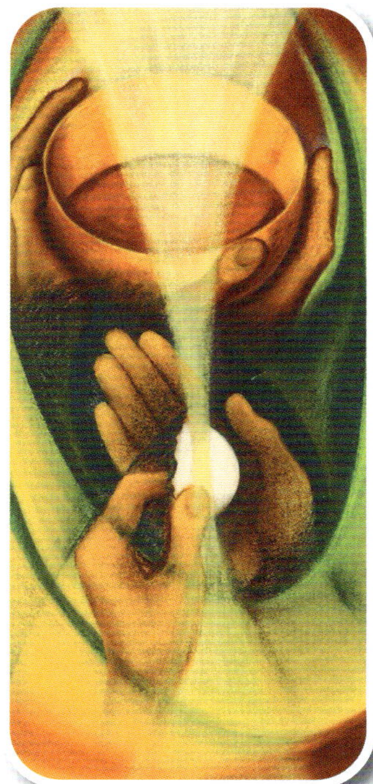

Preparing to receive Jesus

Now, it is the time to receive Jesus. When we see the priest hold up the Host and listen carefully to him say, 'Behold the Lamb of God', we know that Jesus is now coming to us in Holy Communion. We can prepare to receive him by remembering how much he loves us and can tell him that we love him too.

Receiving Holy Communion

When we receive Holy Communion, we know by faith, that it is Jesus we receive. We say, '**Amen**' which is the same as saying, 'Yes, I do believe'.

We welcome Jesus and thank him for coming to us and we talk to him as our very, very best friend.

Knowing that Jesus is present within us, we want to be close to him and receive his love. After communion is a special time for talking to Jesus in our heart. We can thank him for all the blessings he has given us. Jesus wants to help us and to know about anything that might be worrying us.

Activities

1. Write a prayer to welcome Jesus into your heart that you could say before you receive Holy Communion.

2. Remember, Jesus will be very close to you when you receive him in Holy Communion.
   How can you be really close to Jesus? Think of something to help you do this.

At the end of Mass

At the end of Mass, the priest gives a blessing and says:

"Go in peace, glorifying the Lord by your life."

This means that having received Jesus in Holy Communion, we are now able to bring his presence into our home, school, playground, football pitch, in fact, everywhere we go. We become co-workers for Jesus by being kind and thoughtful to everyone we meet.

Activities

1. Another name for Jesus is Lord.
   a) What do you think is meant by 'Go in peace, glorifying the Lord by your life'?
   b) Give an example of how you might do it.

2. Make a pocket sized booklet to help you remember what to do at each part of the Mass:

   - at the beginning;
   - at the Readings;
   - at the Offertory;
   - at the Consecration;
   - at Holy Communion;
   - when Mass is over.

Our Parish Church

Be familiar with your Parish Church.
Reflect on its importance for you.

Inside the Church

Your parish church is a *little bit like* your second home. It is yours, so it is important that you know all about it. Here are some notes to help you.

What does the word 'Church' mean?

It has two meanings:

- All people who have received the Sacrament of Baptism and want to follow Jesus.
- The building where we go to celebrate Mass.

Why is there an altar?

The altar is to remind us of the Last Supper when Jesus handed over his life for us.

Why is there a tabernacle?

The tabernacle is the place where the Blessed Sacrament is kept. People pray before the Blessed Sacrament.

What is the Blessed Sacrament?

Some of the Sacred Hosts which were consecrated at Mass are placed in the tabernacle. These are called the Blessed Sacrament.

What is the meaning of the crucifix?

The crucifix reminds us of the death of Jesus on the Cross by which he offered his life out of love for all people.

Why is there a sanctuary light?

The sanctuary light is to remind us that the Blessed Sacrament is in the tabernacle.

Why does the priest have a special chair?

The priest represents Jesus so he has a special chair when he sits down to listen to the Readings and to pray silently.

Why is there a lectern?

A lectern is a special stand for the Bible. We believe the Bible is the Word of God.

Why do we have statues?

We have statues to remind us of the saints. We do not pray to the statue, but it helps us to remember the saint.

Why do we genuflect when we enter and leave the church?

We genuflect as a mark of respect before the Blessed Sacrament.

Why do we dip our fingers into holy water and make the sign of the cross as we enter the church?

We use holy water to remind us of our baptism.
We make the sign of the cross to remind us that Jesus offered up his life in love on the cross for us.

Activity

Imagine you have been invited to speak about your parish church to pupils of another faith. You can do this with a Power Point presentation or make a guide booklet which you will explain to them as you give your presentation. Try to include some photos.

a) Give the name of the church and your parish priest.

b) You should include the following and give an explanation:
- Altar
- Tabernacle
- Sanctuary light
- Crucifix
- Statue or stained glass window
- Lectern
- Priest's chair

c) Mention some of the important events that take place in your church and reasons for them.

5. Celebrating Easter and Pentecost

Explore how the Church celebrates the Resurrection of Jesus.
Think about how we can celebrate Jesus' Resurrection.

Celebrating New Life

Spring

Winter is over.
The world is waking up
from its deep sleep.

The bare tree is now clothed,
the daffodil raises its golden head,
the sharp wind is conquered by the
gentle breeze.

Once again, the Creator
has restored life to a sleeping world.

Have you ever noticed the changes around us after a long winter? The weather becomes warmer and we don't have to wear gloves, scarves or even jackets as we travel to school in the mornings. The evenings become brighter. The bare trees are gradually covered in leaves. Flowers and plants begin to appear. During springtime, the world begins to wake up from its long winter sleep and come to life again!

Celebrating Easter

At Easter, the Church celebrates a very special feast about coming to life again – **the resurrection of Jesus!**

Easter is the most important feast that we celebrate in the whole year. This is because on Easter Sunday we celebrate Jesus' resurrection from the dead. Even though Jesus suffered and died on the cross, his resurrection shows that God's power is greater than death. God raised Jesus from death to new life!

Activities

1. In silence, take one minute to look at the resurrection picture. Write a short prayer, about five lines, describing the wonderful moment when Jesus rose from the dead. Begin and end your prayer with 'ALLELUIA!'

2. Read the poem 'Spring' on page 70. Answer the following questions.
   a) What signs of new life in spring are mentioned in the poem?
   b) What other signs of new life have you noticed in springtime?
   c) Make a list of all the things you enjoy about springtime.
   d) Who do you think the 'Creator' in the poem is meant to be?
   e) Explain the last two lines of the poem in your own words.

The Easter Vigil

The Easter Vigil begins late on Holy Saturday after night has fallen. The service begins with the lighting of the Easter or Paschal candle from a fire outside. This is to remind us that Jesus, our light, is risen.

The cross on the candle reminds us that Jesus died and rose again to new life. The A and O on the candle are the first and last letters of the Greek alphabet. They remind us that the risen Jesus will live forever.

The Easter Vigil Mass

The Mass is a very joyful celebration. Everyone has a lighted candle as a reminder that Jesus is with us and that He is the light of the world.

All the prayers and readings remind us that Jesus has passed from death to new life. We say:

**We proclaim your death, O Lord,
and profess your resurrection
until you come again.**

Activities

1. In what way is Easter a celebration of new life?

2. As the Paschal Candle is lit, the priest says the following prayer:

   **May the light of Christ, rising in glory,
   dispel the darkness of our hearts and minds.**

   a) Draw a candle in your book and write these words around your candle.
   b) How is Jesus a 'light' to Christians?
   c) How can we be a 'light' to others?

3. Imagine you have been asked to explain Easter to someone who has never heard of this feast. Write a letter using words and pictures. Include the following points:
   - what we celebrate at Easter;
   - why Easter is the most important feast in the Church year;
   - how Easter is celebrated in Church;
   - why the Paschal candle is lit.

Key Words

creator Holy Saturday
Easter Vigil Paschal candle feast

Jesus is Risen

Know that Jesus appeared to some of his disciples on the road to Emmaus.
Think about what we can learn from this experience.

Jesus is Alive!

This account of Jesus appearing to two of his disciples, shows us how their despair changed to happiness when they saw Jesus was truly alive!

A walk with Jesus

Two of Jesus' friends were walking along the road from Jerusalem to a village called Emmaus. They felt sad and confused and talked about all that had happened - how Jesus had died on the cross, how his body had been laid in a tomb and how the tomb had been found empty three days later.

While they were talking, Jesus appeared and walked alongside them but they did not recognise him!

"What are you talking about?" Jesus asked. They looked at him sadly. Then they said, "You must be the only person who has been staying in Jerusalem these past few days and doesn't know what has been going on".

They told Jesus about all the things that had happened, how everyone had hoped Jesus would set them free from the Romans, but instead he had been put to death. They also told him how some women went to his tomb and said it was empty. The women said they had seen angels who said Jesus was alive! Some of their friends had gone to the tomb and found everything exactly as the women had reported, but there was no sign of Jesus.

Jesus said, "O foolish men, why are you so slow to believe that Jesus died and has really risen again?"

Jesus explained to them that all this happened just as the Scriptures said it would. As they listened to him, they began to feel happier.

They drew near to the village and they asked Jesus to stay and have supper with them.

While they were at supper, Jesus took the bread, blessed it, broke it and gave it to them. As he did this, they recognised him. Then, he vanished out of their sight.

They said to each other, 'It was Jesus! He really is alive!' Their hearts were full of joy. They hurried all the way back to Jerusalem to tell Jesus' other friends the good news!

We are told that Jesus 'vanished out of their sight'. The disciples could no longer see Jesus; but they knew he was still with them. They believed he would always be with them. It is the same for us. We cannot see Jesus as we can see other people, but that does not mean he is not there. Because he has risen to new life, Jesus will always be with us.

Activities

1. Work in pairs.
   a) What do you think were some of the questions the disciples might have asked Jesus?
   b) What answers do you think Jesus gave them?

2. Imagine you are one of Jesus' two friends in the story above.
   a) Write down what you told the others when you got back to Jerusalem.
   b) Explain why this experience was so important for you and others.

3. What do you think is the important lesson Jesus wants us to learn from his appearance to the two disciples?
   Why is it important?

Jesus appears to the Apostles

Know what Jesus said to Thomas when he did not believe Jesus had risen from the dead.
Reflect on the meaning of these words for us.

Doubting Thomas

We have seen how happy Jesus' friends were when they realised that Jesus had risen. As well as happiness, they must have felt amazement and wondered how such a thing could be possible.

One of Jesus' special friends was a man called Thomas. He really loved Jesus and when Jesus died, Thomas felt very sad. When Thomas' friends told him that Jesus' tomb was empty and that some of them had actually seen Jesus, he couldn't believe it. He wished it were true. He really missed Jesus but he felt that such a thing was not possible. How could someone who had died be alive again? It just didn't make sense!

Thomas said to his friends, "I will not believe Jesus has risen unless I see him for myself!"

About a week later, Thomas and his friends were in their house with all the doors shut. Suddenly, Jesus appeared in the middle of the room and said, **"Peace be with you".**

Thomas was amazed! He wondered if that could really be Jesus whom he loved so much and thought he would never see again?

Jesus came to Thomas and spoke to him,
"Why do you doubt, Thomas? Can you see the marks on my hands from the nails on the cross? Believe that it is me".

Then, Thomas realised that it really was Jesus and that he had risen to new life. He cried out, "Jesus, my Lord and my God, I do believe!" Jesus replied, **"You believe because you have seen me. Blessed are those who have not seen me and yet they believe in me".**
(John 20:24-29 adapted)

Activities

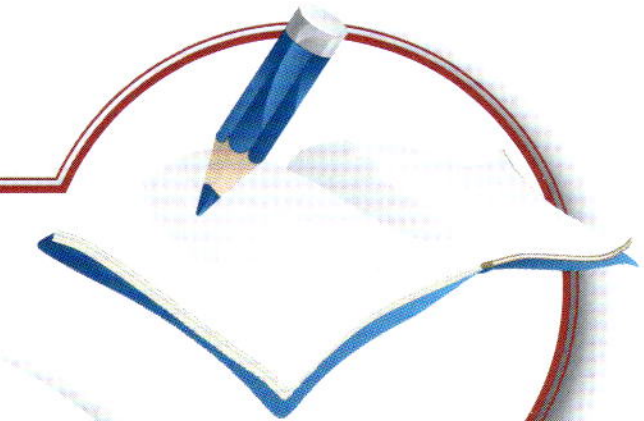

1. Jesus told Thomas:
   **"You believe because you have seen me.
   Blessed are those who have not seen me and yet they believe in me".**
   a) What do these words mean for us?
   b) When might these words help us most of all?

2. Work with a partner. Imagine you are a reporter for the 'Jerusalem Times'. You have been sent to interview Thomas about his experience.
   a) Write a list of questions that you would like to ask Thomas about what happened and how he came to believe in Jesus' resurrection.
   b) Now imagine you are Thomas. Write your answers to these questions.
   c) Use this information to prepare a media presentation. This could be a newspaper article, a TV or radio broadcast or a web announcement.

3. Work in groups.
   a) Choose either the appearance of Jesus to Thomas or to the disciples on the road to Emmaus.
   b) Write this story as a little play.
   Think about:
      - the number of characters will you need;
      - who they should be.
   c) Write down what each person will say.
   d) Choose one person to introduce the story.
   e) Practise your story and then present it to the rest of the class.

The Meaning of the Resurrection

When Jesus rose from the dead, joy and hope came into the world because death is no longer the end of everything.

Jesus' resurrection gives us hope that when we die, God will raise us to new life. We believe we will live forever with Jesus in the kingdom of heaven.

We also believe that Jesus' resurrection gives us hope every day:

- he is always close to us;
- he is looking after us;
- he is offering us the same new life that he has.

Activities

1. Work in pairs. Make a poster for the school entrance or for your church to remind everybody about Easter. Explain:
   a) what happened at Easter;
   b) why Easter is important;
   c) the best way to celebrate it.

2. Make a display of:
   a) the ways the apostles had for spreading the good news of the resurrection;
   b) the variety of ways of doing it now.

The Ascension

Know that Jesus returned to Heaven.
Reflect on what this means for us.

Jesus goes back to Heaven

One day, Jesus told his apostles that he would be leaving them to return to his Father. They were sad but Jesus explained that he was going to prepare a place for them - and for us.

He said:

- **the Holy Spirit will come to you;**
- **he will give you courage so that you will not be afraid to tell people about me;**
- **he will help you to remember all I said.**

Then he told them:

- **to go back to Jerusalem;**
- **to stay in the city until the Holy Spirit came;**
- **that they must be his witnesses so everyone would know that he rose from the dead.**

As Jesus finished speaking, it became very cloudy in the place where they were. The apostles could not see Jesus at all. They were still trying to see into the cloud when they noticed that two men dressed in white were standing there.

Pause to discuss:

The Ascension is a **sad** and a **happy** occasion.
Can you explain why?

The men said:
"Why are you standing there, looking up to heaven? Jesus has gone back to heaven, but one day people will see him return".

The disciples went straight back to Jerusalem and stayed there as Jesus had asked them.
(Acts 1:6-11 adapted)

Every day, they all met together to talk about Jesus and to pray.

Activities

1. a) Think about Jesus' return to heaven and the promises he made to the apostles.
   b) Using the words in the boxes, discuss or write the questions you think the apostles would want answered.

When?	Where?	Why?	How?

2. Reflect on all that Jesus said to the apostles before he left. These words were also meant for us.
   a) What were they?
   b) When will they happen?
   c) What do we have to do?

Celebrating Pentecost

Know what happened at Pentecost.
Reflect on how it changed the apostles.

Needing help!

Have you ever had a problem that you couldn't solve on your own but someone came along and helped you to solve it? Perhaps you had difficulty doing some homework but someone gave you some help. Perhaps you did not understand something in class and a teacher explained it to you. Or, maybe you have helped someone else, for example, lending a hand around the house or cheering up a friend who felt unhappy. The truth is, we all need a helping hand at one time or another!

Activity

a) Write or draw about a time someone gave you help when you needed it.

b) Think of somebody you will meet today. How might you help that person?

c) Why is it important to help one another? (Clue p.38)

Pentecost

The apostles needed help. Jesus had promised to send his Spirit to help them but they did not know when that would happen. They knew they should carry on the work Jesus had begun when he was on earth, but they didn't know how to do it.

Then, one day as they were praying, that help came: Jesus sent the Holy Spirit to be their helper and changed their lives forever!

On the day of Pentecost, Jesus' friends were together in one room. Suddenly, a very powerful wind began to blow. It filled the room with its mighty roar. They saw tongues of fire come down and rest upon their heads. They were all filled with the Holy Spirit and began to speak foreign languages as the Spirit gave them the gift of speech.

Suddenly, they no longer felt unsure about what they should do. They knew their task now was to spread the good news that Jesus had told them.

Activity

The apostles went out to tell everyone they met about Jesus and his teaching.
Take turns to be an apostle in the 'hot seat' and tell the class what you know about Jesus.

The Power of the Holy Spirit

Peter and the apostles went out and began to tell everyone they met all about Jesus and his teachings, the miracles and the wonders he worked.

The crowds were amazed at what they heard. On that very first day, over three thousand people wanted to join them. This was a powerful sign that the Holy Spirit, that is the Spirit of Jesus, was working through the apostles.

Activity

Imagine you were one of the apostles in the room when the Holy Spirit came.

a) Write about what happened - what you saw, heard or felt.

b) Explain how the Spirit changed you and what you did to tell other people about Jesus.

The Feast of Pentecost

Every year, on the feast of Pentecost, the Church remembers how the Holy Spirit was sent to help the friends of Jesus.

This is a very important feast because without the Holy Spirit, the friends of Jesus would never have had the courage or the confidence to carry on the work Jesus had begun. If that had happened, many people like us might never have heard of Jesus.

We can now be sure that the Holy Spirit will help us to be like Jesus and to carry on his work.

Activity

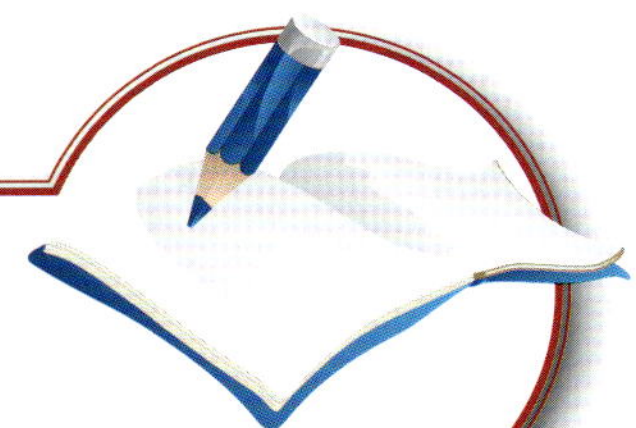

On the day of Pentecost, the Holy Spirit came in the form of wind and tongues of fire.

a) Design a Pentecost banner which includes one or both of these symbols.

b) If you wish you can add some wording to your banner – perhaps choose a line from a hymn to the Holy Spirit.

c) When you have designed your banner, you can make it using different materials.

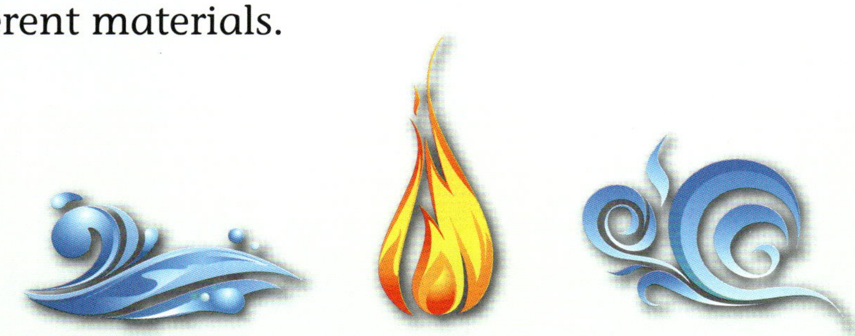

The Fruits of the Spirit

Know about the fruits of the Holy Spirit.
Reflect on times when we need the help of the Holy Spirit.

Fruits

In our country we can find a great variety of fruits, even when they are not in season. They come from all over the world to our supermarkets.

Fruits of the Spirit

St. Paul uses the image of fruits to explain to us the type of help that the Holy Spirit, the Spirit of Jesus, gives us. These fruits are not ones you can buy in the supermarket or pick in the orchard. They are fruits that grow inside us with the help of the Spirit. They are **'love, joy, peace, patience, kindness, goodness, faithfulness, gentleness, self-control'**

These fruits can help us to change just like the friends of Jesus changed on the day of Pentecost.

The Holy Spirit helps Us

St. Paul says that if we let the Holy Spirit work in us, as it worked in Jesus' friends on the day of Pentecost, then, we would have all these good qualities.

Patience

Love

Gentleness

Peace

Self-control

Faithfulness

Kindness

Joy

Goodness

The Holy Spirit came to help the friends of Jesus and that includes you and me! The Spirit is alive in each of us. We know the Holy Spirit is alive in people whenever they do and say things that show God's Spirit of love, joy and peace. Other people know the Holy Spirit is alive in us whenever we act in a kind and caring way.

There are times when we all need a helping hand to be the good Christians we have been called to be. The Holy Spirit is always there to help us. When we find it hard to be kind or to forgive someone we can ask for his help. When we don't want to share with others or let someone join in our games, when we are about to lose our temper or say unkind words - these are all times we can call on the Holy Spirit and ask for help.

Activities

1. a) In the middle of your page write the words,
   The Spirit lives in me when....

   b) Take a whole page of your book to copy the design below.

   c) Think about things that you can do or say that will show others the Holy Spirit is alive in you. Now, write these in the bubbles.

2. a) Draw a flame shape on card and cut it out.
   b) Inside the flame write your own prayer to the Holy Spirit asking for help to be a better person.

3. Work in a small group.
   a) Together, select one fruit of the Spirit, for example 'love'.
   b) Prepare a presentation for the rest of the class on the fruit of the Spirit you have chosen. Explain how it can help you to be a better person.

4. Fruits of the Spirit in my life.
   Choose one fruit for each of the next six weeks and record how you have lived it in your life.

6. Being a Christian

Begin to understand what being a Christian involves.
Reflect on what it means for us.

The Challenge

Being a Christian is not easy. It takes courage – but it's a great adventure! When we really do what Jesus asks us, life is full of surprises and challenges.

Even when there is a lot of suffering, we can help each other like these boys in the photo from East Timor. Their homes have been destroyed in an earthquake but they are helping each other to be brave and to trust in God.

Pause to reflect

To be a Christian we have to:

- love God with all our heart;
- love our neighbour as ourselves;
- be ready to forgive over and over again;
- trust in God no matter what happens.

Jesus shows us the Way

Jesus was kind to everybody. He was always ready to forgive people when they had done wrong. He went about doing what he could to help others: to comfort the lonely, to cure the sick and to work miracles so that people would believe in the power of God.

When Jesus was asked what was most important in order to inherit eternal life, that is, to get to heaven, he explained that there was not just one thing but two:

"'Listen', Jesus said, 'the Lord our God is the one Lord, and **you must love the Lord your God** with all your heart and with all your soul, with all your mind and with all your strength.

The second is this: **You must love your neighbour as yourself**'" (Mark 12:29-30).

Activity

a) Work in pairs. Name all the things that happen in your school to help others.

b) Make a 'Spider Diagram'. Put 'Loving God and Others' in the middle of it. Around the diagram put details of all the ways you help.

Forgiveness

One day, Peter asked Jesus how often he should forgive somebody who has done something wrong to him. Without waiting for Jesus to reply, he said, "'What if that person hurts me again and again, should I forgive him seven times?'" Here is what Jesus said:

> **"Not seven, I tell you, but seventy-seven times" (Matthew 18:22).**

Jesus is telling us that we must always love God, love one another and always be ready to **forgive** each other when we do something wrong.

Activities

1. Work in in groups. Imagine you are the Head Teacher or the Deputy Head. Prepare for a school assembly.
   a) Think of ways to explain to all the pupils what is most important in order to be a follower of Jesus.
   b) Give examples of how to do it.
   c) Give encouragement so that everyone will want to do it. (If you wish you can use photos and make a Power Point presentation.)

2. a) Discuss what you think is happening in this sketch. (Clue: think about forgiveness).
   b) Now, copy it into your book and write a script to go with it.

Loving My Neighbour

Know what Jesus teaches about helping others.
Reflect on how we help others.

Who is my Neighbour?

One day, Jesus was asked to explain what we have to do in order to get to heaven. Jesus replied that we have to love God and love our neighbour. Then he was asked, 'Who is my neighbour?'

"Jesus replied, 'A man was once on his way down from Jerusalem to Jericho and fell into the hands of robbers; they took all he had, beat him and then made off, leaving him half dead.

Now a priest happened to be travelling down the same road, but when he saw the man, he passed by on the other side. In the same way, a Levite (a person who helps priests with their work) came to the place, saw him, and passed by on the other side. But a Samaritan traveller who came by was moved with pity when he saw him.

He went up and bandaged his wounds, pouring oil and wine on them. He then lifted him on to his own donkey, carried him to the inn and looked after him.

Next day, he took two denarii (enough money to pay for him) and handed them to the innkeeper. ‘Look after him,’ he said ‘and on my way back I will make good any extra expense you have.’

‘Which of these three, do you think, proved himself a neighbour to the man who fell into the robbers’ hands?’ ‘The one who took pity on him,’ replied the man. Jesus said to him, **‘Go, and do the same yourself’**” (Luke 10:29-37).

Activities

1. List five things the Good Samaritan did to help the man who was attacked by robbers.

2. Sometimes people say we should be ‘Good Samaritans’.
   a) What do you think it means?

   b) Give examples of ways we can be ‘Good Samaritans’:
      - in school;
      - at home.

3. Discuss. What do you think are the links between being a Christian and being a ‘Good Samaritan’?

4. Do you think it is easy to be a Christian? Why? Why not?

St. Paul

Know how St. Paul had to learn to be a Christian.
Think about what we can learn from his experience.

Saul becomes Paul

There was once a man called Saul who did everything he could to hurt Christians. He thought that they were just troublemakers and he did not believe in the teachings of Jesus. One day, he set off on a journey to the town of Damascus searching for Christians. He wanted to arrest them and throw them into prison.

As he drew near to Damascus, a brilliant light suddenly shone all around him and he heard a voice say to him, **"Saul, Saul, why do you persecute me?"** Saul was bewildered and asked who it was. The voice replied, **"I am Jesus and you are persecuting me. Get up now and go into the city and you will be told what to do."**

The light disappeared but Saul was left blinded – he could see nothing! His friends took him by the hand and led him to a house in the city.

After a few days, a Christian called Ananias came to visit him and healed his blindness. Saul had realised that it was Jesus who had spoken to him on the road to Damascus. He also understood that in persecuting Christians, he was persecuting Jesus because Jesus is present in Christians, in each one of us. He wanted to become a Christian so Ananias baptised him there and then. (Acts 9:1-19 adapted)

From that day on, Saul changed from being an enemy of Jesus to being one of his greatest followers. To show that he was no longer the man he had once been, he changed his name to Paul. Before long, he became an apostle and spent the rest of his life spreading the good news of Jesus!

Activities

1. **Hot-Seating:** Imagine you are the Jewish Leaders who want to interview Saul.
   You have heard that he has become a Christian.

   Preparation: Work in pairs to plan the questions before the interview. Saul and a companion should think of answers.

2. St. Paul wrote many letters to Christians explaining Jesus' teachings to them. Here is part of one of his letters to Christians who lived in the town of Corinth:

   "Love is patient and kind.
   Love is not jealous or boastful.
   It is not arrogant or rude.
   Love does not insist on its own way.
   It is not irritable or resentful."
   (1 Cor. 13: 4-6)

   a) Think about what each line in this letter means.

   b) Choose one line of this letter.
   Give an example to explain the meaning of it.

3. Imagine you are Saul. Design a 'WANTED' poster for Christians. Explain why you want them captured and what 'crime' they have committed.

4. News headlines: **Convert or Traitor?**
   a) Find out what these words mean.
   b) Which do you think is the right one for Saul? Why?
   c) Explain the reason for the change in Saul's character.

Meeting Jesus

Know that the Sacraments are a meeting with Jesus.
Be aware that in the Sacraments we receive Jesus' great love.

Meeting Jesus in the Sacraments

To be close friends of Jesus means that we must try everyday to be kind and helpful to those we meet. This is not always easy; sometimes it is very difficult, so we need help!

We are going to think about how, in each of the sacraments, we meet Jesus in a special way and also receive his help for our daily lives.

In the **Sacrament of Baptism**, we enter into the life of Jesus and become members of the Church.

When we are baptised, we become Christians and receive Jesus' help for our journey through life.

In the **Sacrament of Reconciliation**, we have the chance to say 'sorry' to Jesus for the wrong choices we made and to start again.

In the Sacrament of Reconciliation, that is, when we go to Confession, Jesus forgives us for anything we have done wrong. No matter how often we fail, he offers us the grace to change our lives and start again. We can receive the Sacrament of Reconciliation every time we have done anything wrong and want his help.

In the **Sacrament of the Eucharist**, Jesus comes to us in Holy Communion.

At Mass, when we receive Holy Communion, Jesus becomes truly present in us so that we are able to talk to him about anything that worries us and ask for his help. We can tell him that we really want to stay very close to him.

Receiving the Sacraments

Read what these children have to say about the sacraments they have received.

My happiest memory this year was the day I made my first Holy Communion. I received Jesus for the very first time. This made me very happy and I know Jesus will always be my friend. All my family came with me to the Church because they knew it was a very special day for me.

Susan, age 8

On the day I went to confession for the first time, I was really nervous but I was excited as well. I was scared that I wouldn't remember what to say. But the priest helped me and afterwards I felt so happy. Now, whenever I go to confession, I feel happy again.

Stefan, age 7

When I received Holy Communion for the very first time, I felt loved. I thought it was like Jesus was giving me a present when he gave me himself in the form of bread and wine.

Barney, age 7

For these children, their happiest day was the day they received a sacrament for the first time. In every sacrament we receive, Jesus offers us the gift of his life and love. This is the grace we need to help us on our journey through life.

Every time we receive a sacrament, we are reminded that Jesus is with us. He will never leave us!

Activities

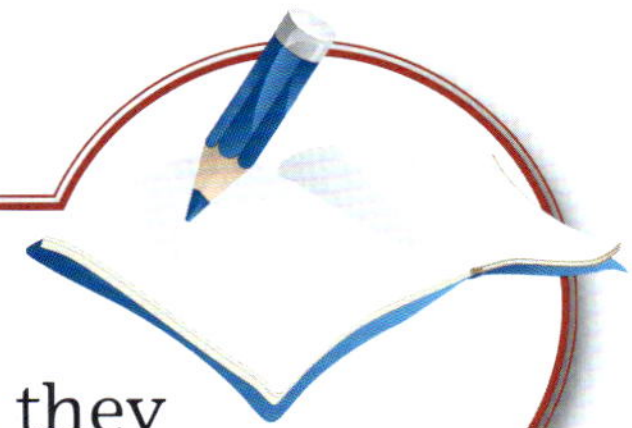

1. a) Why were Susan, Stefan and Barney so happy when they received the Sacraments?

   b) If you have made your first Holy Communion, describe how you felt that day.

2. End of year in school is usually a time for your parents to receive a school report.

   a) Write a report about yourself for Jesus.
   (Tell Jesus about the most important events in your life in the last year.)

   b) Think of ways to thank Jesus each day.

3. Explain how the Sacraments of Baptism, Reconciliation and Eucharist help you to be a close friend of Jesus and to be kind and thoughtful to others.

Using Our Gifts to Help Others

Know about people who use their gifts to help others.
Think about what we can learn from them.

Living a Christian life

One day Jesus warned his friends: "It is not those who say to me, 'Lord, Lord', who will enter the kingdom of heaven, but the person who does the will of my Father in heaven" (Matthew 7:21-22).

This means that we have to 'live out' what Jesus has taught us. We have to put it into practice every day! This is what Dominic Savio did.

St. Dominic Savio

Dominic Savio was born on 2 April 1842 at San Giovanni di Riva, near Turin in Italy. When he was seven years old, he made his First Holy Communion.

Then, he wrote this plan for his life:

I will go to Confession and receive Holy Communion often.

I will keep Sundays and feast days as holy days.

I will have Jesus and Mary as my best friends.

I would rather die than sin.

When Dominic was twelve years old, he went to the Oratory School in Turin. He made friends quickly with the other boys. They admired him because he was always willing to help them with their work and he was particularly kind to anyone who was sick. Most of all, he was a great peacemaker. Whenever he saw boys fighting, he would help them to become friends again.

Dominic's school was beside a church so he would try to find a little time every day to pop in to make a visit to the Blessed Sacrament. He never forgot that Jesus and Mary were his best friends.

When Dominic was only fifteen years old, he became very ill and died on 9 March 1857. Dominic's friends were the first to realise that he was a saint. They began praying to him and many said that he answered their prayers.

In 1954, Dominic Savio was canonized; that means that the Church stated that he was a saint.

Activities

1. a) Make notes on what you admire most about Dominic Savio.
   b) Share your notes with the rest of the class.

2. Why do you think Dominic Savio became a saint?
   (You may like to use the 'Thinking map' in the Teacher's Book p109)

3. Write down three ways you would like to be more like Dominic Savio.

4. Research.
   a) Find out what it means to make a visit to the Blessed Sacrament.
   b) Would you be able to make a visit to the Blessed Sacrament? Why? Why not?

St. Gemma Galgani

St Gemma was born on 12 March 1878 in a small Italian town near Lucca. Gemma always remembered the day she made her First Holy Communion. She said it was impossible to describe what happened, but she had a very strong feeling that Jesus had come to her. She wanted to stay very close to him forever.

Gemma had a very special love for people who were poor. When she went out, they would come to her for help. She often gave them food from her home.

Gemma's dad died when she was quite young. Her family became very poor. She had seven brothers and sisters and she had to help to look after them.

When she could no longer afford to give food to the poor people, she gave them her love and friendship.

No matter what difficulties Gemma had, she would talk to Jesus about them. It was when she received Jesus in Holy Communion that she got the strength, courage and love to be able to help others.

Gemma Galgani died of a serious illness in 1903. She was canonized on 2 May 1940.

Pause to reflect

Slowly, re-read the account of St. Gemma and think about her. Take time to talk to her and ask her to help you.

Activities

1. a) Make a list of things you think were very hard for Gemma.
   b) Who do you think helped Gemma?
   c) There are times when life is hard for us. Is there anything Gemma did that you think would help you? Explain.

2. a) If you had met Dominic Savio or Gemma Galgani in the street, would you have known they were Catholics? Why? Why not?
   b) If you had known either of them as a friend, what beliefs or values would you say inspired their lives?
   c) How did this affect their behaviour?

Prayer

Begin to understand the importance of prayer.
Think about different ways of praying.

Keeping in touch

Everywhere we go we see people keeping in touch, for example, by phone, email or text. Almost every year, there are new ways of keeping in touch.

Keeping in touch with Jesus

The most important thing in our life is to keep in touch with Jesus. Everyday, we should try to stay close to him, to talk to him, to ask for his help and most of all to love him.

How do we learn to pray?

We can pray at any time and in any place. Prayer is opening our heart to Jesus. It is Jesus who wants to give us his life, his love, himself. Jesus is always coming to us, so what we have to do is to open our heart to him. The more we open our hearts, the better we pray.

Opening our heart to Jesus is something we learn to do more and more all our life long. All of us are a bit selfish but the more we can get away from thinking just about ourselves and open our heart to Jesus, the closer he will be to us.

Preparation for Prayer

Everyday, we should try to find a time and place where we can be alone with Jesus, so that our relationship with him grows. We may want a picture of Jesus or something to remind us that he is with us.

- We sit alert but relaxed.
- We breathe slowly and let our eyes close gently.
- We open our heart to Jesus and let him know that we want him to be with us.
- We believe Jesus will listen to what we share with him and he will give us his love and help.

Praying with a Gospel Text

Another way to pray is to choose a text from a Gospel. Imagine you are in the story with Jesus. Slowly bring into your mind:

- what you see;
- what you feel;
- what you hear;
- what Jesus says to you;
- what you say to Jesus.

Slowly read the following account of the Ten Lepers, ten men who could not live with their families because of an illness called leprosy.

The Ten Lepers

"Now on the way to Jerusalem, Jesus travelled along the border between Samaria and Galilee. As he entered one of the villages, ten lepers came to meet him. They stood some way off and called to him, 'Jesus! Master! Take pity on us.'

When Jesus saw them he said, 'Go and show yourselves to the priests'. Now as they were going away they were cleansed. Finding himself cured, one of them turned back praising God at the top of his voice and threw himself at the feet of Jesus and thanked him. The man was a Samaritan. This made Jesus say, 'Were not all ten made clean? The other nine, where are they? It seems no one has come back to give praise to God, except this foreigner.' And he said to the man, 'Stand up and go on your way. Your faith has saved you'" (Luke 17:11-19).

Pause to reflect

Imagine you were there with the Ten Lepers.

a) What did you see?
   What did you feel?
   What did you hear?
   What did Jesus say to the leper who thanked him?
   What do you think the leper did next?

b) What do you think Jesus is asking you to remember from this event? How can you live it out?

Jesus teaches the disciples to pray

One day, the disciples who often saw Jesus praying, asked him to teach them to pray. He replied, "Say this when you pray:

Father, may your name be held holy,
your kingdom come;
give us each day our daily bread,
and forgive us our sins,
for we ourselves forgive each one who is in debt to us,
and do not put us to
the test" (Luke 11:2-4).

In this picture, we can see that Jesus became very still. He may have even closed his eyes so that he was thinking only of his Father. Then, he taught his disciples to pray.

Think about the meaning of this special prayer.

"May your name be held holy."
May we always remember that you are our God.

"May your kingdom come."
May your kingdom of love and trust come into our world.

"Give us this day our daily bread."
Please give us enough to eat today.

"Forgive us our sins."
Forgive us for the times we have made wrong choices and hurt others.

"Forgive us as we ourselves forgive each one who is in debt to us."
We ask God to forgive us in the same way as we are willing to forgive those who hurt us.

"Do not put us to the test."
God knows that we try to be good and not make wrong choices. But we also ask God not to let us be tempted to do things that are wrong.

Activities

1. The **'Our Father'** we usually say is based on the words Jesus used when he taught the disciples to pray. Which text do you prefer? Why? (Use the copy your teacher will give you to compare them.)

2. Imagine you are asked to explain to a new pupil the meaning of the **'Our Father'**.

   Make notes around the copy your teacher gives you to explain what you are going to say to the new pupil.

Glossary

Absolution	In the Sacrament of Reconciliation when the priest, in the place of Jesus, 'absolves', forgives, our sins
Act of sorrow	A prayer to say how sorry we are for our sins
Angels	They live with God in heaven, singing His praise; some are sent as messengers, like Gabriel
Angel Gabriel	The angel whom God sent to Mary
Annunciation	When the angel Gabriel brought God's message to Mary that He wanted her to be the mother of His son, Jesus
Anointed	To bless someone with special oil
Ash Wednesday	The first day of Lent, when we receive the ashes on our foreheads
Baptised	When a person receives the Sacrament of Baptism, they become a Christian
Baptismal candle	The candle given to the newly baptised child
Baptismal font	The place in a church containing the blessed water poured onto someone when they are baptised
Baptismal garment	The white dress or shawl which is put on or wrapped around a newly baptised child during baptism
Baptismal promises	The promises which the parents and godparents make for the child during baptism
Baptismal water	The holy water used to baptise someone
Bible Readings	Usually short stories from the Bible which are read in church, for example, during Mass
Bishop	He is the successor of the Apostles. He is in charge of all the people and churches in his diocese
Celebrate	To rejoice and be happy, and to do something special
Christ	It is another word for Messiah; both mean 'Anointed One'
Christian Name	The name you receive when you are baptised, and usually is a person's first name

Confession	In the Sacrament of Reconciliation when you tell the priest your sins
Creator	A name given to God because He is the one who has made or 'created' everything
Crucifix	A cross with the figure of Jesus on it
Denied	To have told a lie, say the opposite of the truth on purpose
Easter Sunday	The day when Jesus rose from the dead
Easter Vigil	The night before Easter Sunday, when Christians celebrate the death and resurrection of Jesus
Eternal Life	The life with God in heaven which Christians hope to have forever after they die
Eucharist	Another word for the Mass; it comes from a Greek word meaning 'giving thanks'
Feast	A special day when Christians celebrate something important in Jesus' life, or Mary's life, or one of the saints.
Forgiveness	When someone forgives someone else, pardons or lets them off
Fruits of the Spirit	Gifts from God
Genuflect	To go down on the right knee, as a sign of reverence, for example before the tabernacle in Church
Godparent	Someone who promises to help bring up a baptised person as a Christian
Gospel	This means 'good news', and is the story of the life of Jesus
Grace	A help or gift which comes from God
Hail Mary	A prayer to Our Lady, Mary the mother of Jesus
Heaven	Where God is, with Jesus, Mary and all the saints
Holy Communion	The bread and wine that has been changed into the body and blood of Jesus, which we receive at Mass

Holy Saturday	The day before Easter Sunday
Holy Spirit	Third Person of the Blessed Trinity
Inn	A place where travellers could have food and rest
Jews	The 'people of Israel'. These are God's chosen people and their story is in the Bible
Lent	Forty days of preparing for Easter. Lent starts on Ash Wednesday
Lenten promise	A promise to change for the better, which we can make at the start of Lent
Lord	It is a title used for God and sometimes for Jesus
Mary Magdalene	One of Jesus' followers
Mass	The Sacrament of the Eucharist
Oil of catechumens	A sign of strength and healing
Oil of chrism	A symbol of being chosen for a special task in life
Parish	The area Catholics live in where they have their Church and a priest to look after them
Parish church	The Church in your parish where you go to Mass and receive the sacraments
Parish priest	The priest who is in charge of a church and the Catholics in a local area
Paschal candle	The large candle which is lit at Easter
Persecute	Ill-treat
Prophet	A holy person in the Bible, who wrote down or told people all about God
Reconciliation	The sacrament we receive when we confess and receive forgiveness for our sins
Pope	A successor of St. Peter and Bishop of Rome

Repent	To be sorry for the wrong things we have done and to want God's forgiveness
Resurrection	When Jesus, who had died, was raised up to new life by God his Father, on Easter Sunday
Rite of Baptism	The words and signs used when a person is baptised
Sabbath	The holy day in every week when the Jews rest from work and bless God (a Saturday)
Sacrament	A very important gift from Jesus, when we receive special help and grace
Sacred	This means holy or special to God
Saviour	A name given to Jesus, because he died and rose again to 'save' everyone from sin and death
Scripture	Another word for the writings in the Bible
St Paul	A famous follower of Jesus; He died for being Christian
Statue	A carved figure of a person
Swaddling clothes	Clothes to wrap around a new born baby
Tomb	A place where someone is buried
Visitation	The time when Mary went to visit her cousin Elizabeth
Wise Men	Also known as the 'Magi' or 'Kings', they made a very long journey to visit the baby Jesus
Worship	To adore, respect, praise

Acknowledgments

Second and extensively revised edition: July 2011

A joint enterprise by:
Teachers' Enterprise in Religious Education Co. Ltd and Sr Marcellina Cooney CP

Nihil obstat: Father Anton Cowan – Censor.

Imprimatur: The Most Reverend Vincent Nichols PhL, MA, Med, STL
Archbishop of Westminster
29 June 2011 – Feast of SS. Peter & Paul

The *Nihil obstat* and *Imprimatur* are a declaration that the books and contents of the DVD ROM are free from doctrinal or moral error. It is not implied that those who have granted the *Nihil obstat* and the *Imprimatur* agree with the contents, opinions or statements expressed.

Theological Advisor: Fr Herbert Alphonso SJ

Picture Research: Sr Marcellina Cooney CP & Ian Curtis

Acknowledgements
Considerable thanks are due head teachers of the following primary schools for making it possible for their teachers to comment on the text as it developed:
Holy Ghost, Balham SW12; St. Boniface, Tooting SW17; St. Joseph's, Wandsworth SW15; St. Vincent's, Barnet NW7; St. Patrick's, Rochdale OL12 and Vita et Pax, Independent, Barnet N14;

Permission credits
Cover illustration © Jenny Williams; pages 8, 42 & 63 © Mille Images d'Eglise by Jean-François Kieffer; pages 9 & 58 photos © St. Patrick's Primary School, Rochdale; page 10 & 26 photos © St. Vincent's Primary School, Barnet; pages 12, 13, 15, 16, 64, 67, 68, 70, 72, 87 photos © Sr. Marcellina Cooney CP; page 14 photos © Serafina Conboy; page 27 stained glass window © CWS Design; used throughout © venimo/Shutterstock.com, page 5 © Mushakesa/Shutterstock.com, page 6 © Accent/Shutterstock.com, used throughout © rodho/Shutterstock.com, page 8 © Linda Bucklin/Shutterstock.com, used throughout © Francesco Cusmai/Shutterstock.com, page 15 © Aija Lehtonen/Shutterstock.com, page 19 © Michaela Steininger/Shutterstock.com, page 23 © Robert J. Daveant/Shutterstock.com, page 19 © iQoncept/Shutterstock.com, page 20 © Holly Kuchera/Shutterstock.com, page 22 © Zvonimir Atletic/Shutterstock.com, used throughout © balein/Shutterstock.com, page 27 © cobalt88/Shutterstock.com, page 28 © Itana/Shutterstock.com, page 29 © TyBy/Shutterstock.com, page 30 © Vanessa Nel/Shutterstock.com, page 30 © Alberto Pérez Veiga/Shutterstock.com, page 31 © Basheera Designs/Shutterstock.com, page 31 © Sergej Razvodovskij/Shutterstock.com, page 37 © Joel Calheiros/Shutterstock.com, page 51 © PaintDoor/Shutterstock.com, pages 52, 53 & 98 photos © Lorenzo Lees; pages 54 Jesuits Yearbook 2011, page 81 © Elenamiv/Shutterstock.com, page 86 © Danylchenko Iaroslav/Shutterstock.com, page 90 Jesuits Yearbook 2004, page 91 Jesuits Yearbook 2007 & 2009 used with permission from Giuseppe Bellucci, SJ; pages 57 and 66 by Elizabeth Wang © Radient Light; pages 49 & 65 © Sr. Mary Stephen CRSS and McCrimmon Publishing Co. Ltd; pages 71, 84 & 104 photos from St Aloysius Catholic Church, Phoenix Road, London NW1 taken by Sr Marcellina Cooney with permission of Rev James McNicholas PP; page 80 photo stained glass window in St. Colmcille Catholic Church, Kingsland, Coalisland, Co. Tyrone photo by Susan Lawless and used with permission of Rev B Fee PP; page 62 © ITV Global Entertainment, page 104 © Dereje/Shutterstock.com.

Published by
Teachers' Enterprise in Religious Education Co Ltd
40 Duncan Terrace, London N1 8AL

Printed in the UK by Cambrian Printers Ltd, www.cambrian-printers.co.uk